Mel Bay's
LEFT HAND STUDIES
FOR CLASSICAL GUITAR
by Walt Lawry

© 2008, 1983 BY MEL BAY PUBLICATIONS, INC., PACIFIC, MO 63069.
ALL RIGHTS RESERVED. INTERNATIONAL COPYRIGHT SECURED. B.M.I. MADE AND PRINTED IN U.S.A.
No part of this publication may be reproduced in whole or in part, or stored in a retrieval system, or transmitted in any form
or by any means, electronic, mechanical, photocopy, recording, or otherwise, without written permission of the publisher.

Visit us on the Web at www.melbay.com — E-mail us at email@melbay.com

INTRODUCTION

<u>LEFT HAND STUDIES FOR CLASSICAL GUITAR</u> is a book of exercises and studies designed to develop left hand technique. The book concentrates on eight different technical areas;

- chords and chord changing skills
- barres
- shifts
- slurs
- scales
- intervals
- extensions
- left hand harmonics

The text is divided into two parts; a section of exercises and a section of study pieces. The exercises are grouped according to the skill areas they concentrate on and are accompanied by explanatory notes. Most of the study pieces concentrate on two or more skill areas. For that reason the particular skill areas for each piece are listed both in the Table of Contents and at the beginning of the piece itself. Study pieces can be easily matched to exercises, and vice versa. The pieces themselves consist of music written originally for guitar, and of transcriptions.

This book is dedicated to William K. Bledsoe, in appreciation for all his valuable help and advice.

Walt Lawry

TABLE OF CONTENTS

	Page
LEFT HAND POSITION	5

EXERCISES

	Page
STRING CROSSING AND CHORD CHANGE EXERCISES	7
BARRE EXERCISES	11
SHIFTING EXERCISES	14
SLUR EXERCISES	16
SCALE EXERCISES	21
INTERVAL EXERCISES	23
EXTENSION EXERCISES	30
HARMONIC EXERCISES	42

STUDY PIECES — STUDY AREAS

Piece	Composer	CHORDS	BARRES	SHIFTS	SLURS	SCALES	INTERVALS	EXTENSIONS	HARMONICS	Page
ANDANTINO	F. SOR	X	X							48
GRAZIOSO	M. GIULIANI	X	X							50
ALLEGRO	M. GIULIANI	X	X							51
PRELUDE	F. TARREGA	X	X	X						53
GRAZIOSO	M. GIULIANI	X	X	X						54
ANDANTINO	M. GIULIANI	X	X	X						55
MODERATO	F. SOR	X	X	X						57
MODERATO	F. CARULLI	X	X	X						58
ANDANTE	L. BEETHOVEN	X	X	X						60
ANDANTE MOSSO	M. CARCASSI	X	X	X						61
FOLIA DE ESPANA	F. TARREGA	X		X						63
VIVACE	M. GIULIANI	X	X	X						64
PRELUDE NO.20	F. CHOPIN	X	X	X				X		65
PRAYER	F. SOR	X	X	X						66
SARABANDE	J.S. BACH	X	X	X				X		67
BOURREE	J.S. BACH	X	X	X						68
ANDANTINO	M. GIULIANI		X		X					69

		CHORDS	BARRES	SHIFTS	SLURS	SCALES	INTERVALS	EXTENSIONS	HARMONICS	Page
MODERATO	D. AGUADO		X	X	X					70
DOLCE ESPRESSIVO	M. GIULIANI			X	X					71
ANDANTE	M. CARCASSI		X	X	X					72
LARGO	F. SOR		X	X	X					73
CANARIOS	G. SANZ			X	X					74
VALSE	F. SOR		X	X	X		X			77
STUDY	F. TARREGA	X	X	X	X					78
ALLEGRO	M. CARCASSI	X	X	X		X				79
ALLEGRETTO	M. CARCASSI		X	X		X		X		81
ALLEGRO	F. TARREGA		X	X		X				83
MINUET	J.S. BACH		X			X		X		84
MINUET IN A	F. TARREGA		X	X	X	X				85
MARCH	J.S. BACH		X	X		X				86
ALLEGRO	F. SOR						X			87
EXERCISE	F. CARULLI			X			X			88
ALLEGRETTO	N. COSTE			X			X			89
ANDANTE	F. SOR			X	X		X			90
MUSETTE	J.S. BACH		X				X			91
PRESTISSIMO	M. GIULIANI		X	X			X			92
STUDY	D. AGUADO		X			X		X		93
ENDECHA-OREMUS	F. TARREGA	X	X	X				X		94
PRELUDE	J.S. BACH	X	X	X				X		95
AU CLAIR DE LA LUNE	M. CARCASSI			X					X	98
MARCHE	F. SOR			X					X	99
MENUET	F. SOR	X	X	X				X	X	100
MARCHE	F. SOR	X	X	X				X	X	101
ANDANTINO GRAZIOSO	M. CARCASSI	X	X	X	X	X	X	X		103
MODERATO	F. SOR	X	X			X		X		104

LEFT HAND POSITION

Good left hand position makes any piece of music easier to learn. To develop a good left hand position;

1. Only the left hand fingertips (except for barres) and the tip segment of the thumb should contact the neck. The other parts of the hand should be clear of the neck.
2. The thumb should contact the neck opposite the fret played by the second finger. (This can change when doing extensions).
3. The whole length of the finger should be above the level of the fretboard.
4. The fingers should always remain curved, with no collapsed joints (except for the first finger during some barre chords).
5. The wrist should always be bent as little as possible.

Here follow some photographs illustrating good and not-so-good left hand technique.

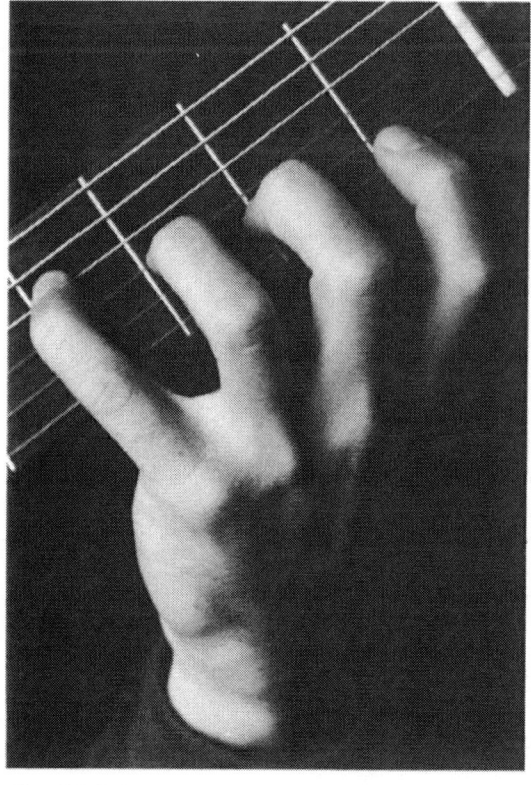 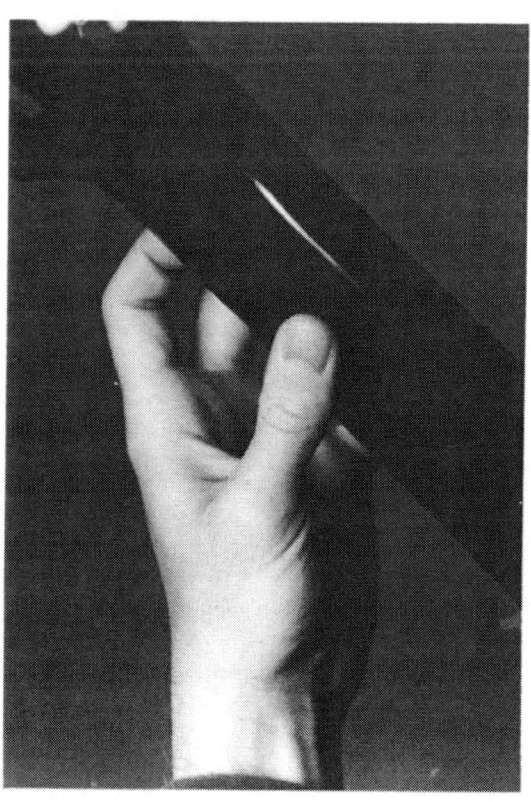

Good left hand position; front view. Good left hand position; rear view.

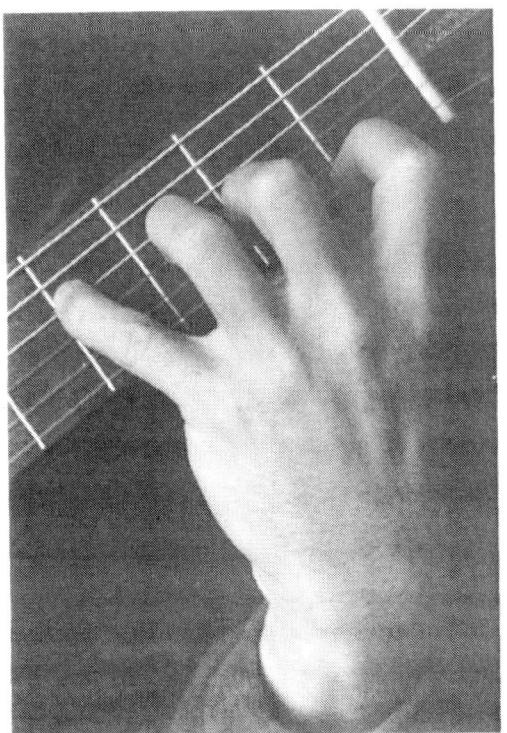

Not good; too much bend in wrist.

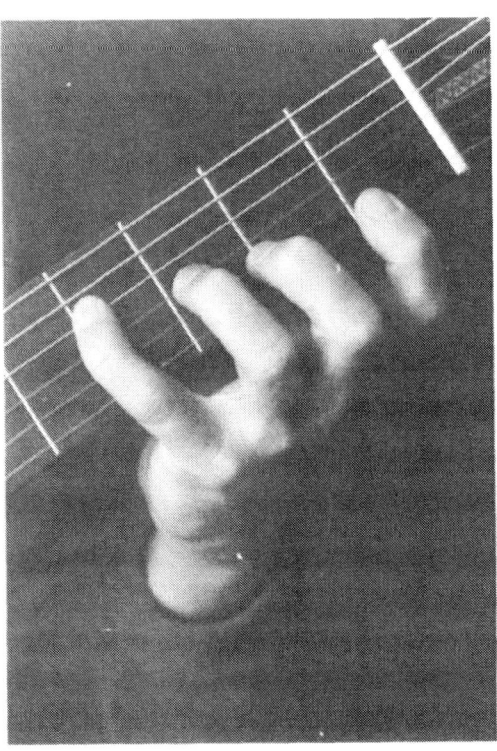

Not good; knuckles below level of fretboard.

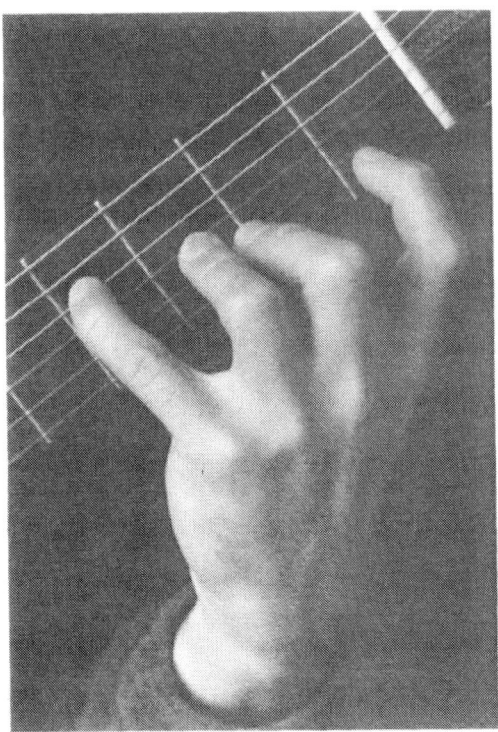

Not good; knuckles collapsed.

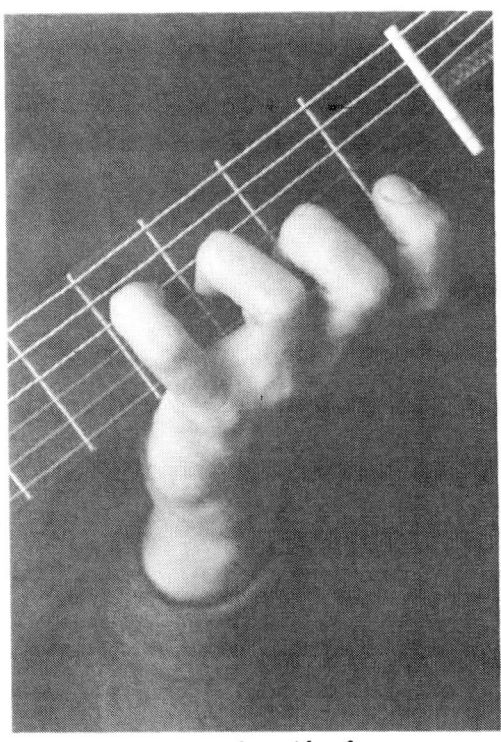

Not good; palm touches side of fretboard.

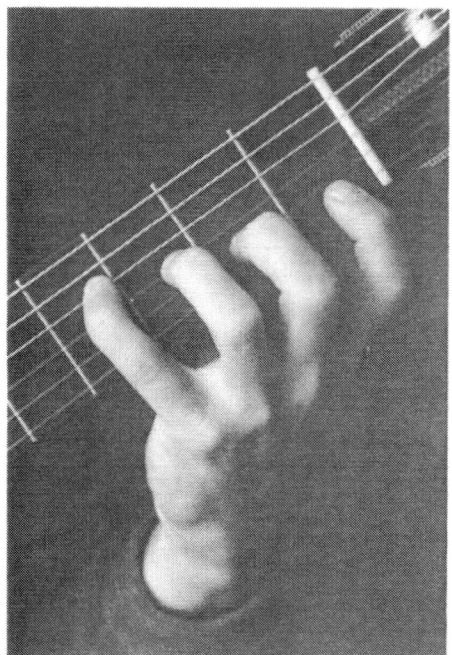
Not good; fingertips contact strings too far from frets.

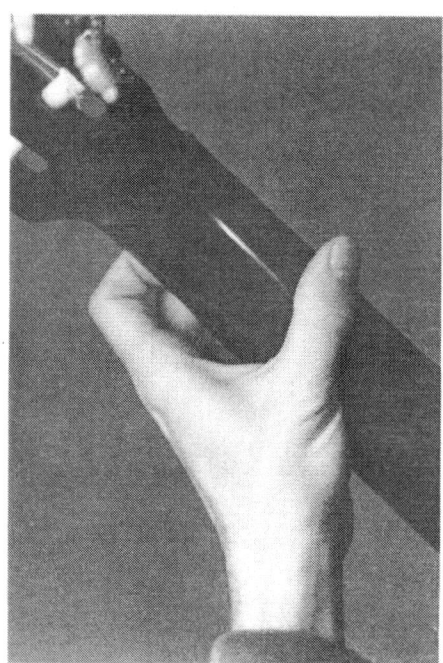
Not good; thumb wrapped around neck.

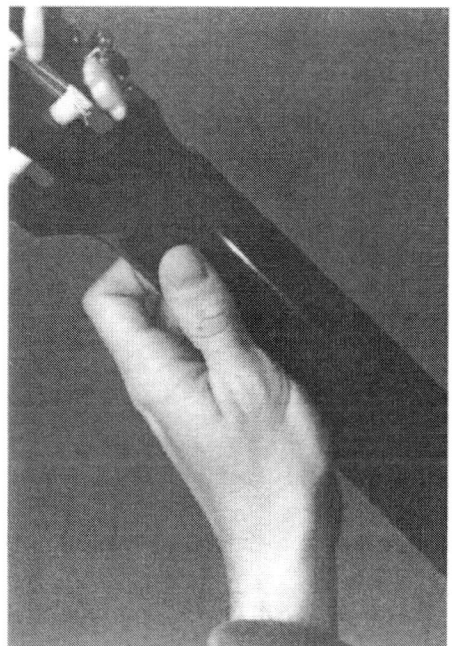
Not good; all of thumb is in contact with the neck.

STRING CROSSING AND CHORD CHANGING EXERCISES

These exercises are designed to develop the skills necessary to do quick and accurate chord changes. Try to keep all the movement in the fingers. Move the rest of the hand and the wrist as little as possible. Use slow tempos at first.

Ex. 1 (a-c) Chromatic octaves. For developing finger independence and agility.

Ex. 1

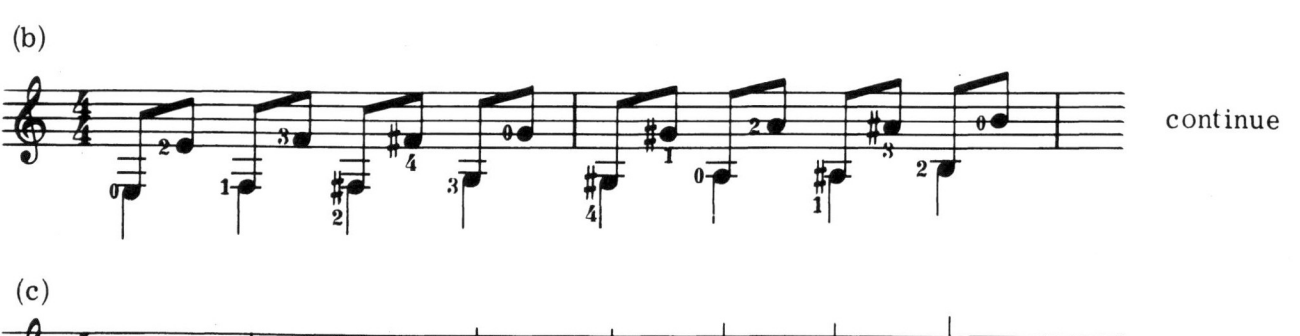

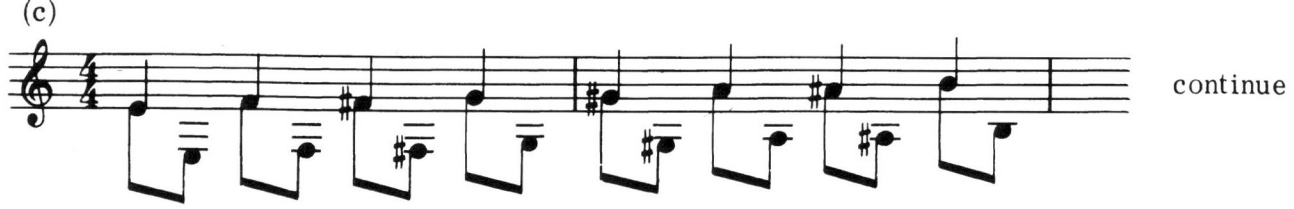

Ex. 2 (a-f) String crossing exercise to develop the accuracy of different finger combinations.

Ex. 2

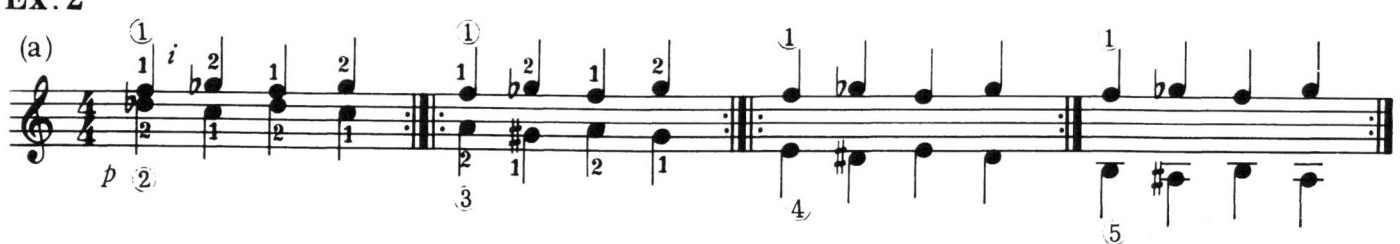

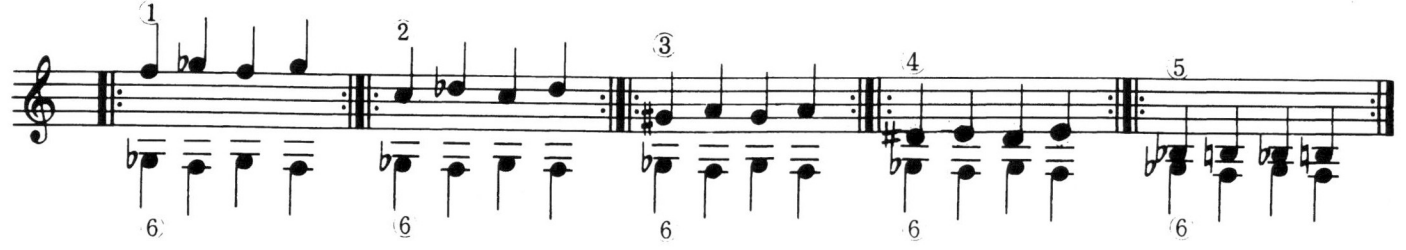

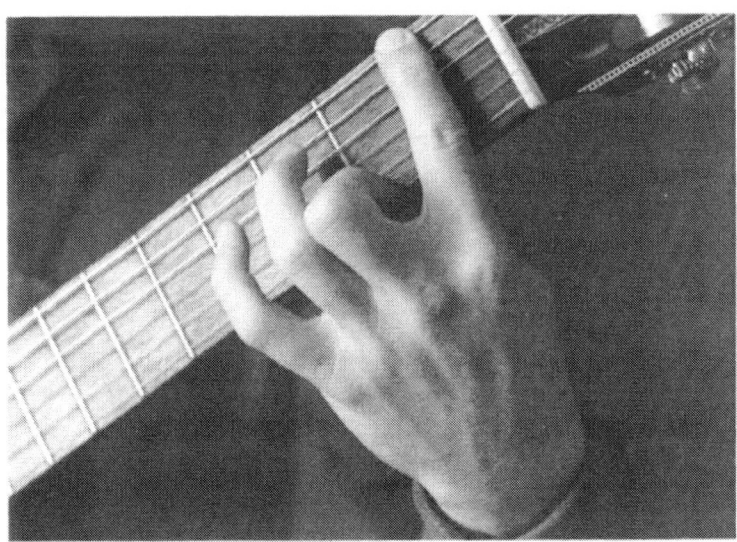

Measure 5. Good; most movement is in the fingers. Wrist moves as little as possible.

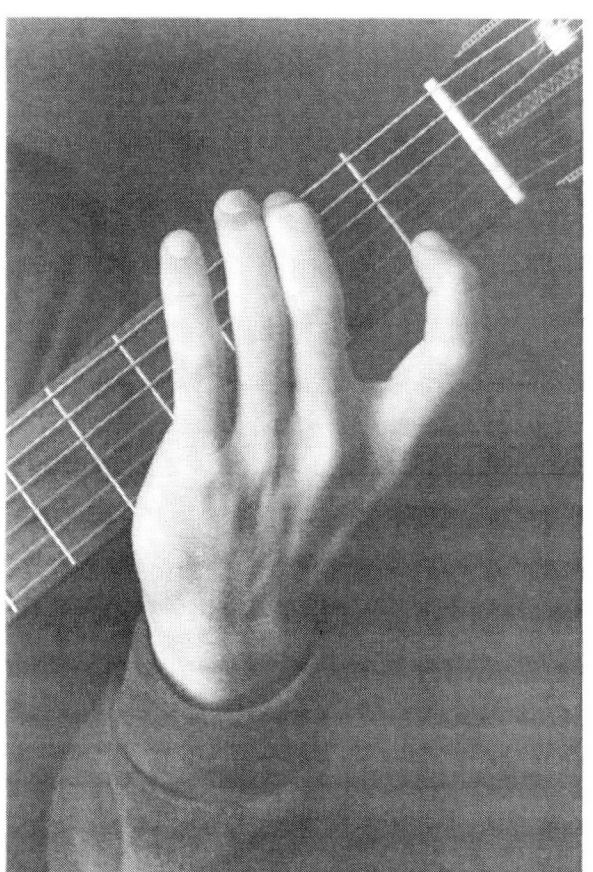
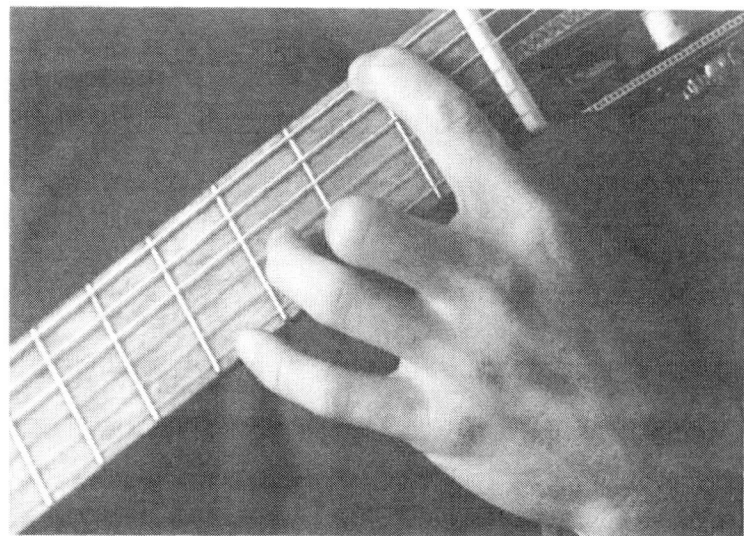

Measure 5. Not good; too much wrist and arm movement. Compare with page 9.

Ex. 3-5 **Chord** change exercises. In each measure one note of the chord drops one half-step lower. For developing quick and accurate finger movements. Continue each exercise until you reach first position.

Ex. 3

continue to first position

Ex. 4
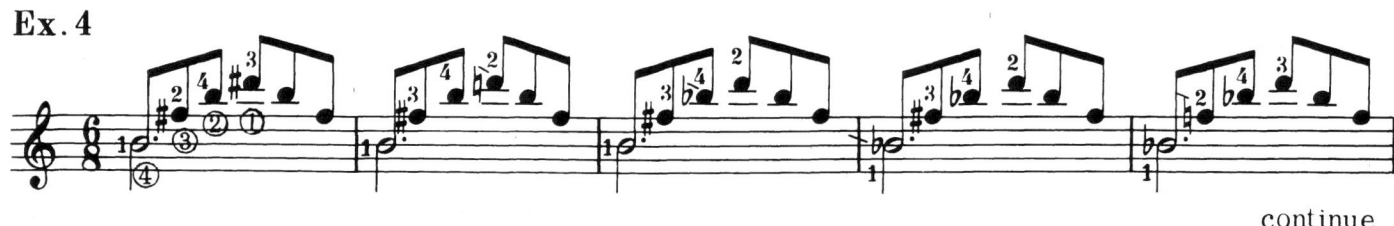

continue

Ex. 5
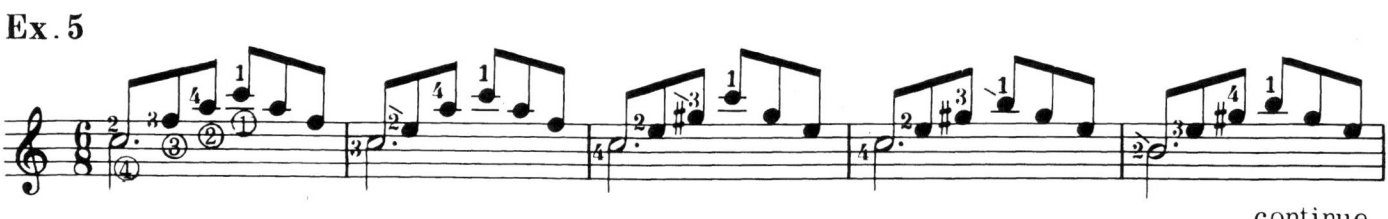

continue

BARRE EXERCISES

Play these exercises only until the muscles in the left hand start to ache, then stop. The strength needed to perform barres must be built up over a period of time. Forcing the left hand to do too much can injure those muscles you are trying to develop.

Ex.1 - to develop strength and accuracy in the first finger. Place the barre as close to the fret as possible without muffling the sound. When exercise is comfortable, start in eighth position and move down one fret at a time without stopping.

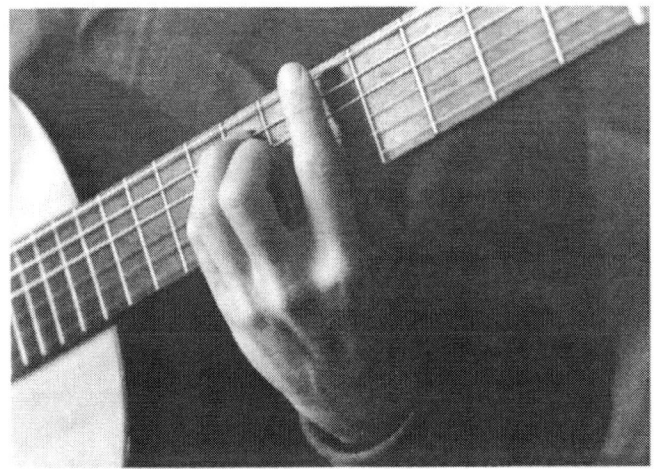

Barre off.

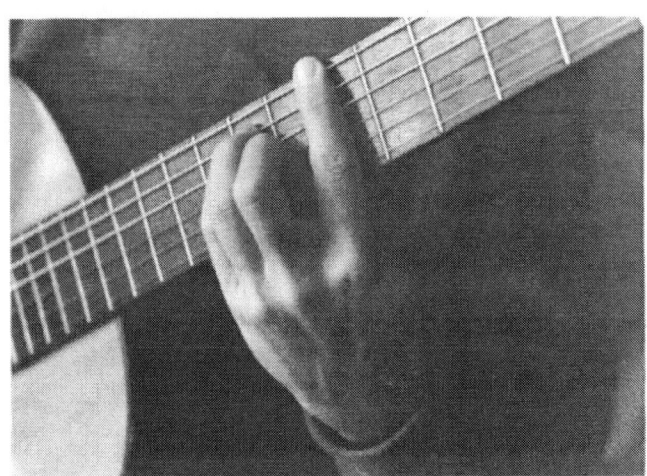

Barre on.

Ex.2 - to develop the different partial barres. Practice in other positions as well. See pg. 12.

11

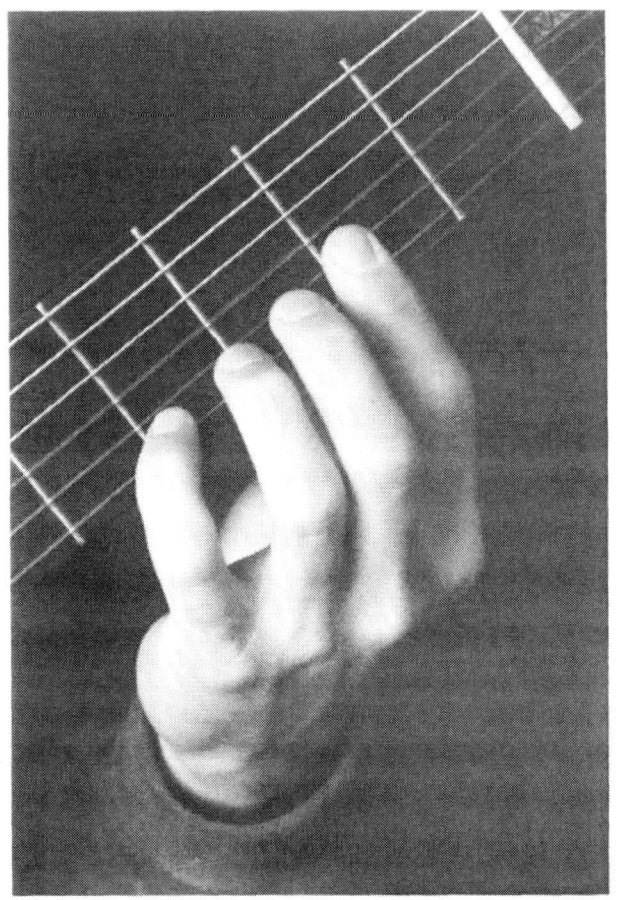

1/3CII

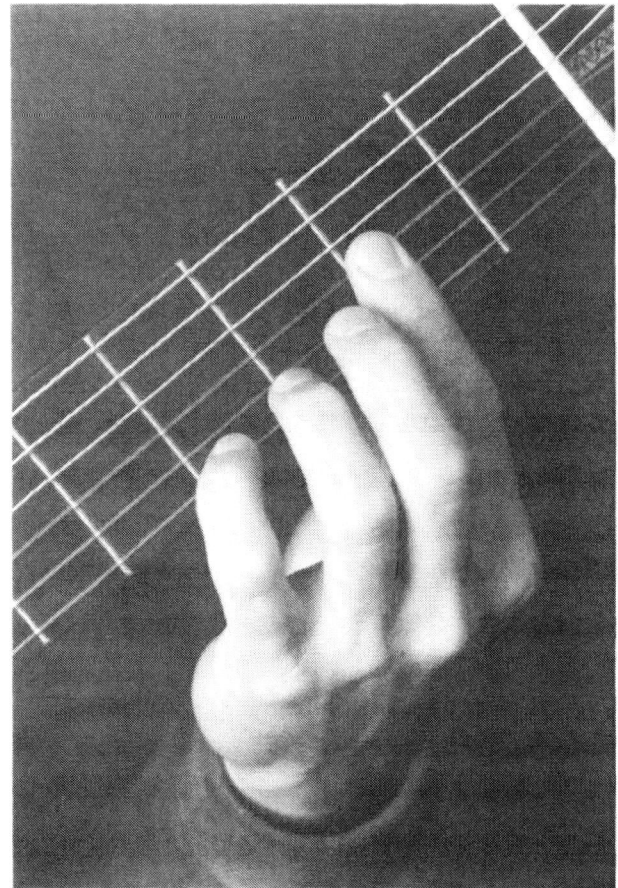

1/2CII

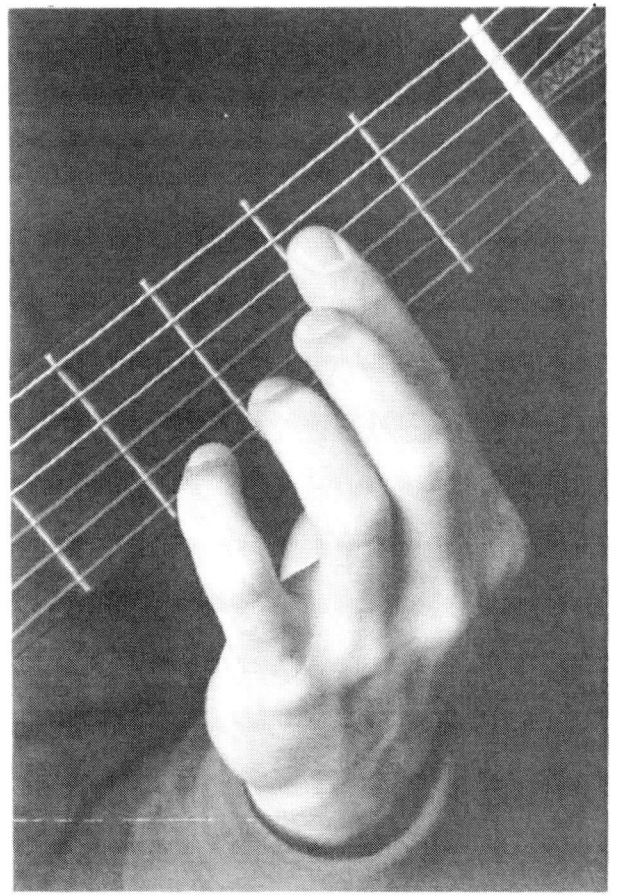

2/3CII

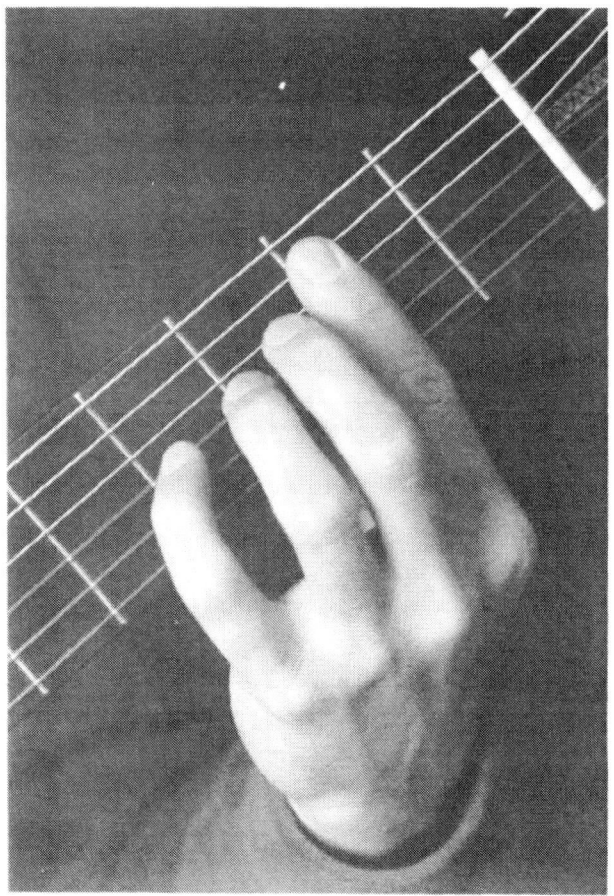

5/6CII

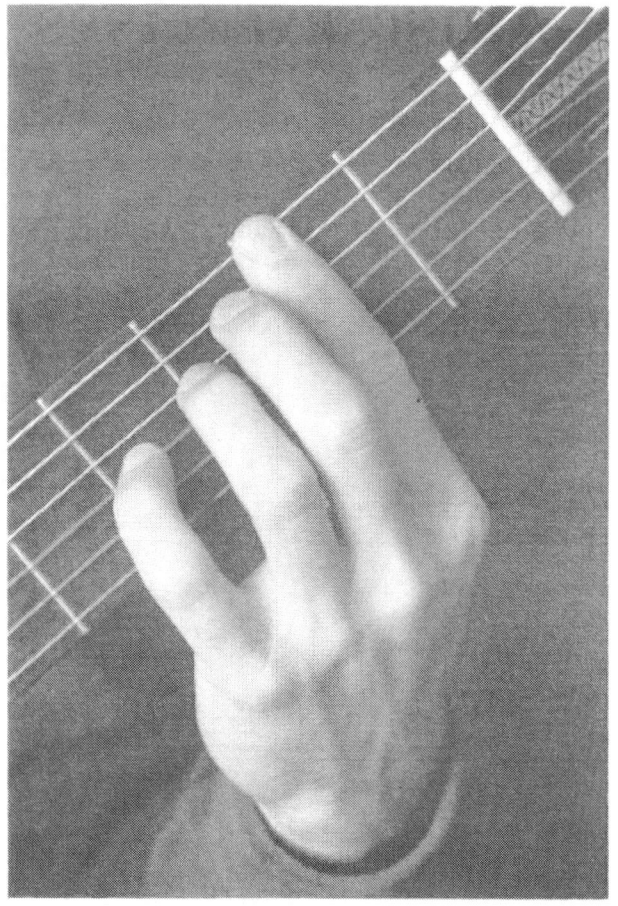

CII

Ex.3 - to increase the independence of fingers 2, 3, and 4 when a full barre is being held. Practice in different positions.

Ex.4 - to develop the ability to play different chord forms while holding a full barre. When comfortable, play exercise in first position and then move up one position at a time without pausing.

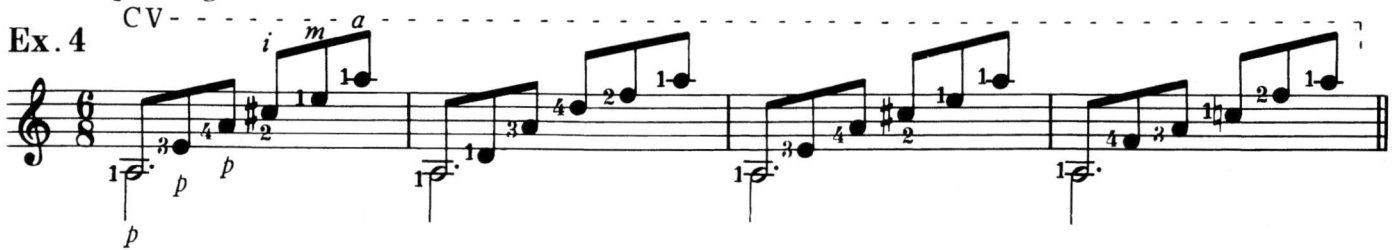

SHIFTING EXERCISES

Shifting involves three separate movements of the left hand;

1. Release pressure.
2. Shift hand to new position.
3. Re-apply pressure.

Be sure to practice these exercises slowly enough to do the shifts properly, especially in Exercises 4-6. If the sound "slides" with your finger during a shift, it is an indication that there is still pressure on the string.

Ex. 1 (a-f) One fret shifts using different finger combinations. The lower finger should always Remain in contact with the string. Do not lift it when using the upper finger. Release pressure when shifting.

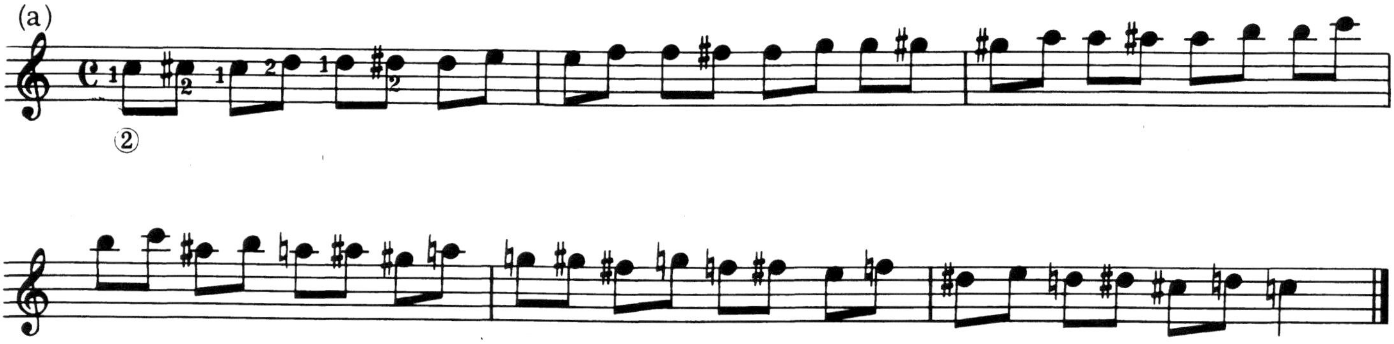

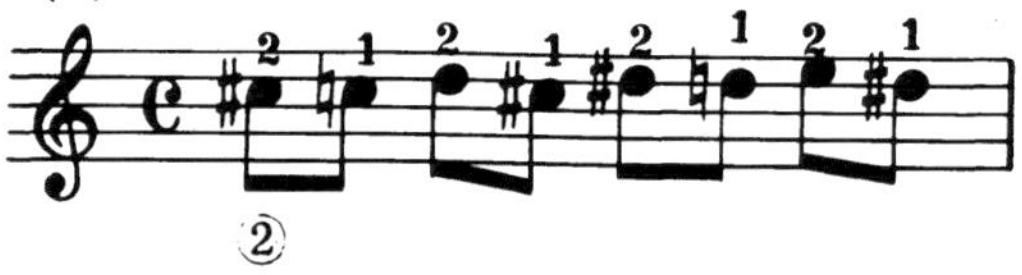

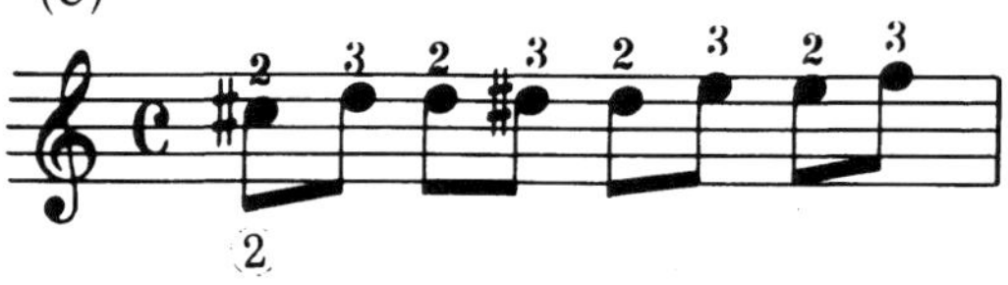

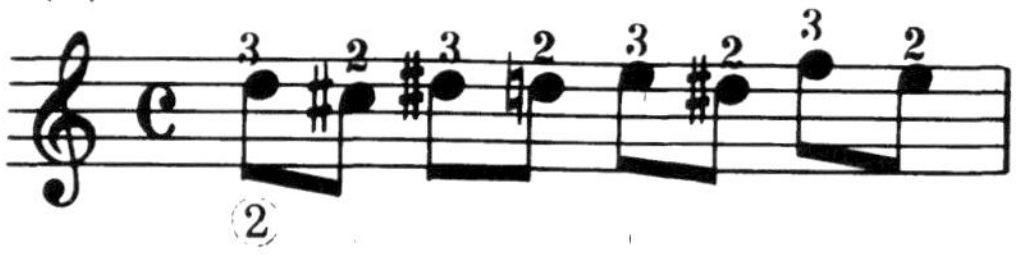

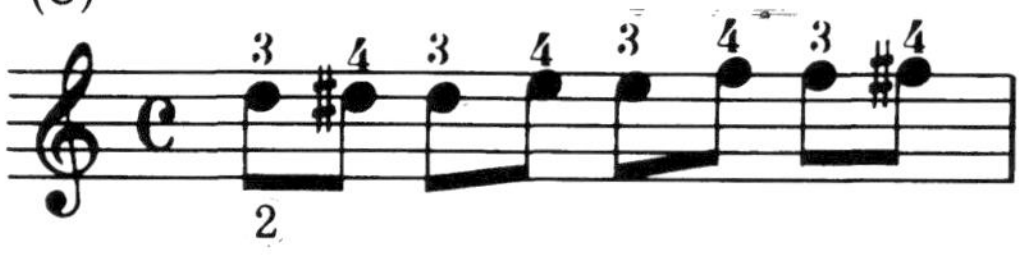

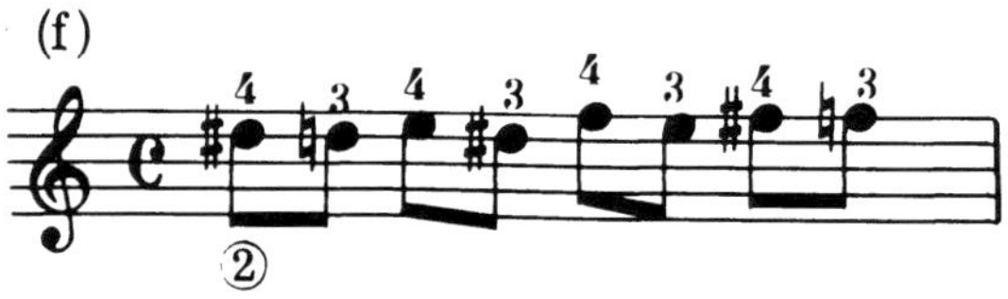

Ex. 1

(a)

(b)

continue

(c)

continue

(d)

continue

(e)

continue

(f)

continue

Ex. 2 (a-d) Two fret shifts using different finger combinations. Follow the pattern given by Ex. 1(a).

Ex. 2

(a)

continue

(b)

continue

(c)

continue

(d)

continue

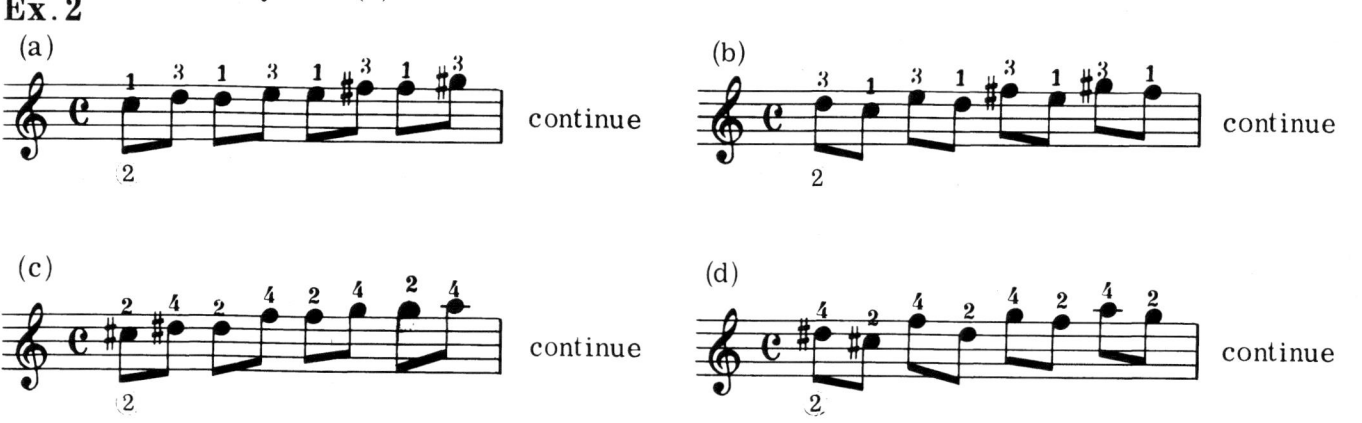

Ex.3(a-b) Three fret shifts using fingers one and four.

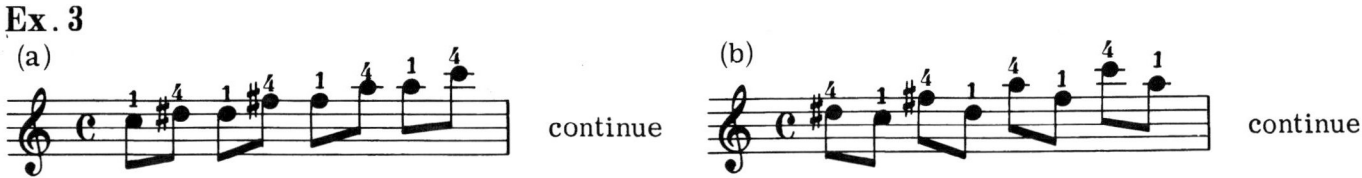

Ex.4 Diatonic scale using one finger on one string. Requires constant one and two fret shifts.

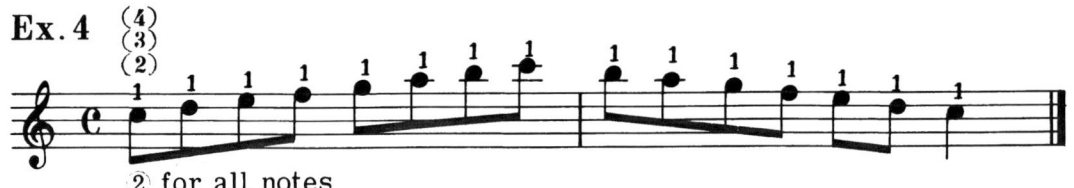

Ex.5 (a-d) Progressive shifting exercise for developing accuracy and concentration. Use a slow tempo.

Ex.6 One string major scale. Practice also on strings two and three.

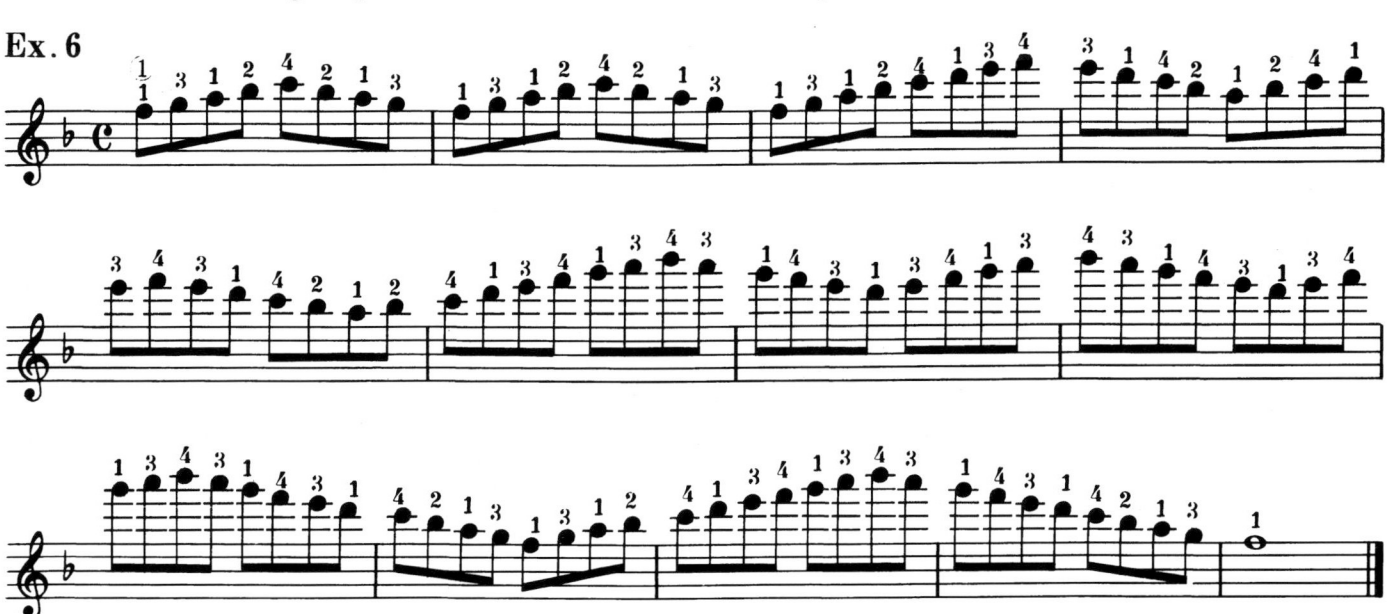

SLUR EXERCISES

Ex. 1 (a-d) For left hand alone; right hand does not play. Place finger as indicated by note in parentheses. Pluck the string with that finger to produce the sound of the second note. Action is similar to right hand rest stroke. In (b-d) the second note should remain fingered throughout the exercise. Do each exercise on all strings. Make sure the fingers do all the work. The rest of the hand and the wrist should not move.

Ex. 1

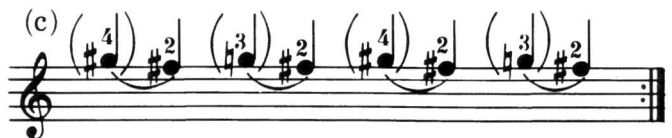

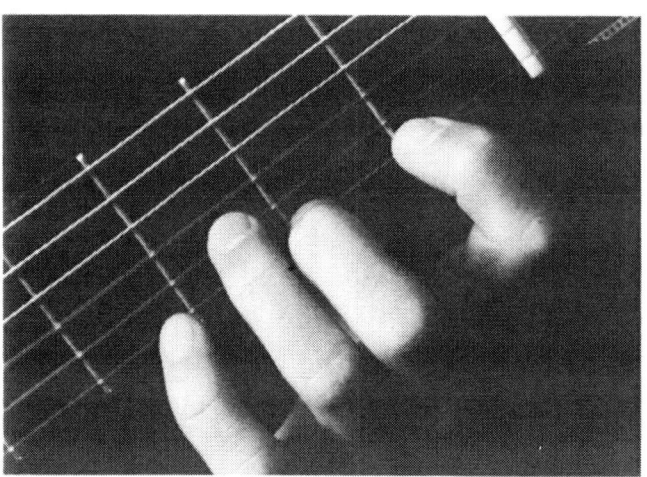

Ex. 1(b): 2-1 slur. Start. Good.

Completion. Good; all movement in finger.

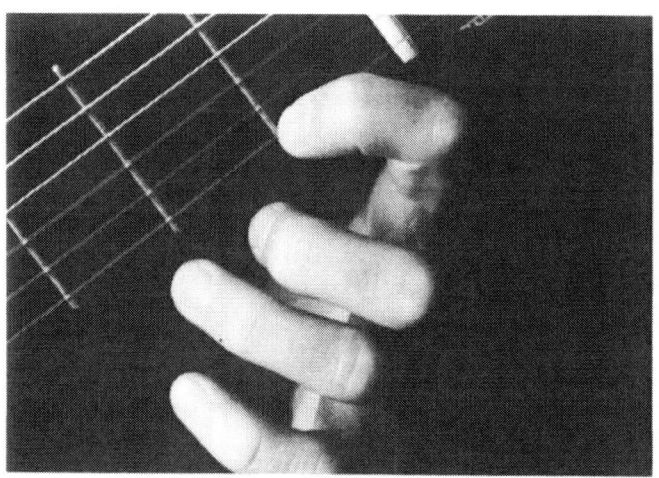

Completion. Not good; hand has pulled away from the neck.

Ex. 2 (a-d) Reversal of Ex. 1. To produce second note, fingers should "hammer" straight down and contact the string just behind the fret. Practice on all strings.

Ex. 2

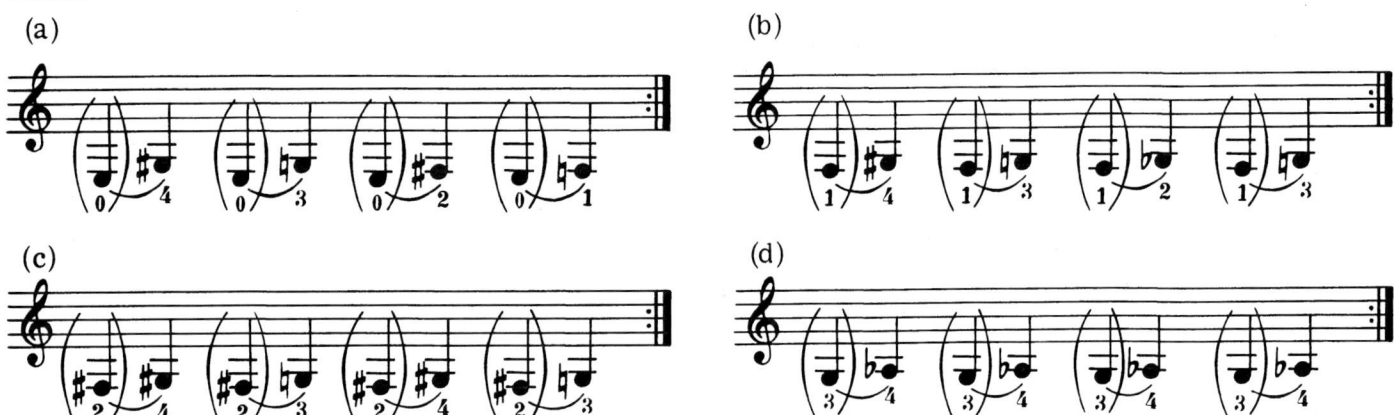

After the left hand action has been developed, Exercises 1 and 2 should be played with the first note of each group plucked by the right hand.

Ex.2(b): 1-2 slur. Start. Good; hand in position, second finger above fret.

Start. Not good; hand pulled back out of position. Compare.

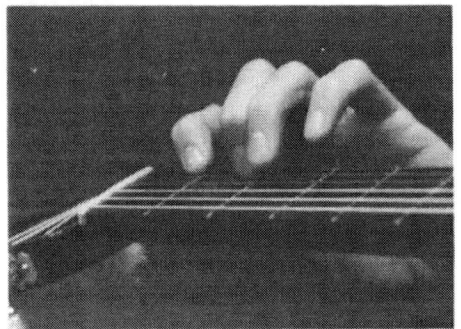

Completion. Good.

Ex. 3 (a-b) For practicing the different finger combinations. Play as indicated.

Ex. 3

Ascend to ninth position, descend to first position. Repeat on each string.

Ascend to ninth position, descend to first position. Repeat on each string.

Ex. 4 - 14 To develop strength and stamina in the left hand. All exercises are played in the manner of Ex.4. Especially good for developing the third and fourth fingers. Slurs of two, three, four, five and seven notes are included.

Ex. 4

continue to ninth position

continue to ninth position

continue to ninth position

Ex. 5

(a)  (b) 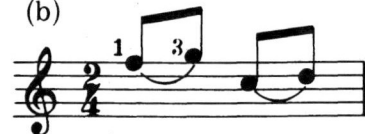 (c)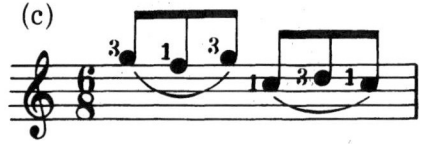

Ex. 6

(a)  (b)  (c)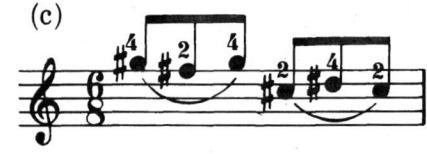

Ex. 7

(a) 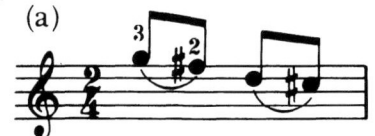 (b) 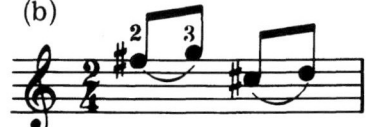 (c)

Ex. 8

(a) 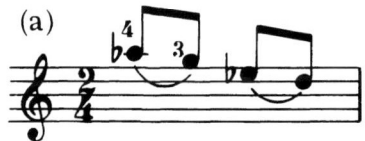 (b) 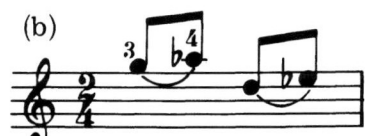 (c)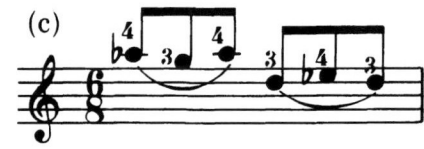

Ex. 9

(a)  (b) 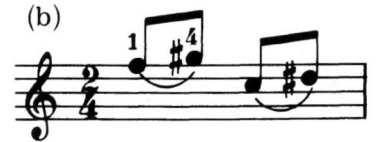 (c)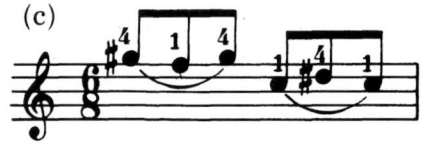

Ex. 10

(a)  (b)  (c)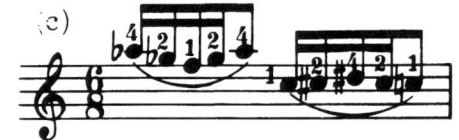

Ex. 11

(a)  (b)  (c)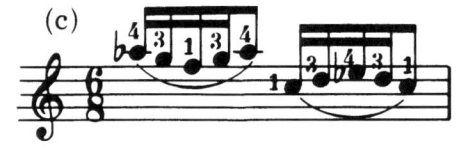

Ex. 12

(a) 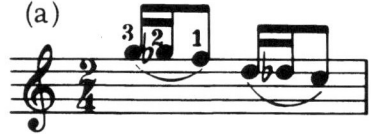 (b)  (c)

Ex. 13

(a)  (b) 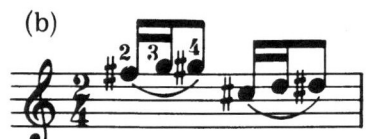 (c)

Ex. 14

(a) 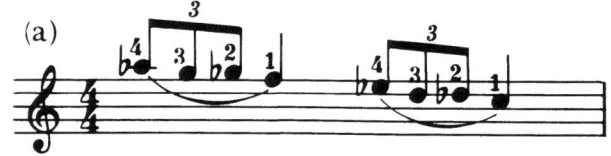 (b)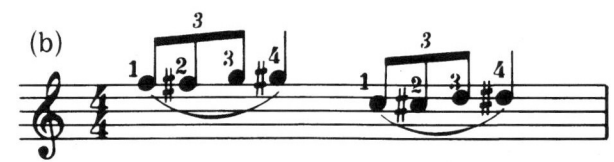

(c)

SCALE EXERCISES

These major and minor scales are all in closed form; they use no open strings. These forms can be moved to various positions along the neck in order to cover the different keys. Three types of scales are represented; scales with extensions, scales with shifts, and normal scales where no extensions or shifts are required.

Ex. 1 - 2 Normal major scales No shifts or extensions required.

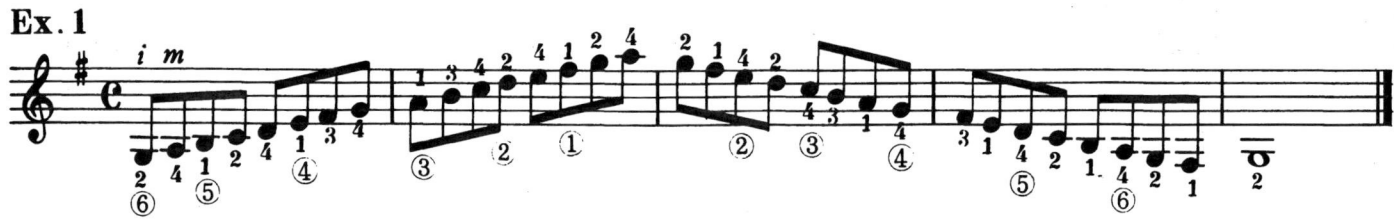

Ex. 3 - 5 Major scales where the extension of the first finger is required.

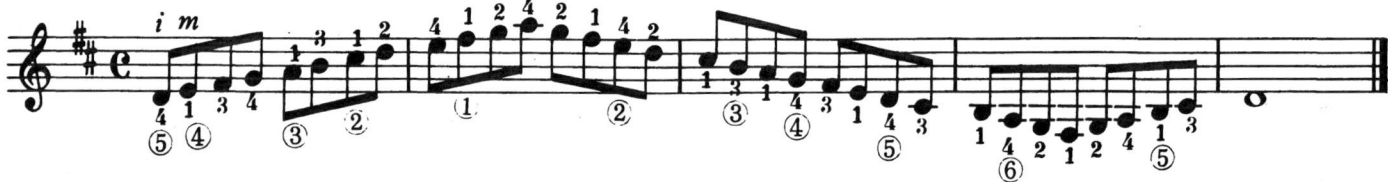

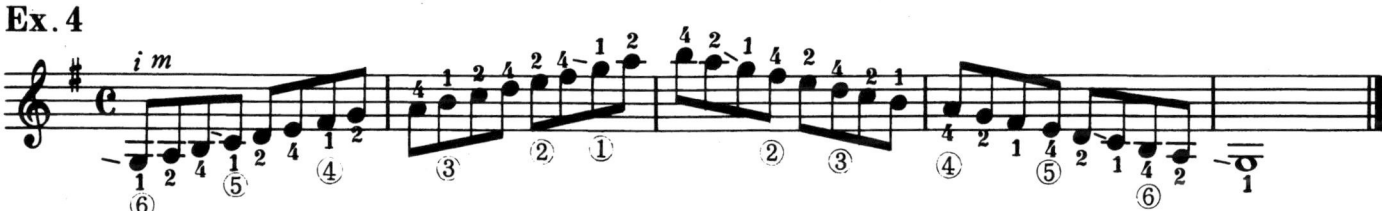

Ex. 6 Major scale where the extension of the fourth finger is required.

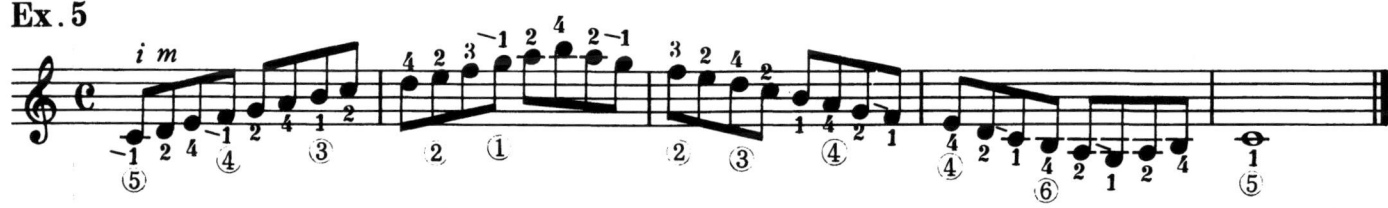

Ex. 7 - 8 Major scales which require shifts.

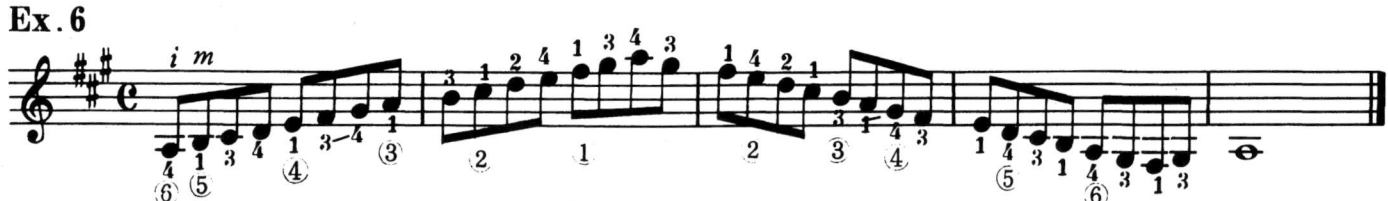

Ex. 8

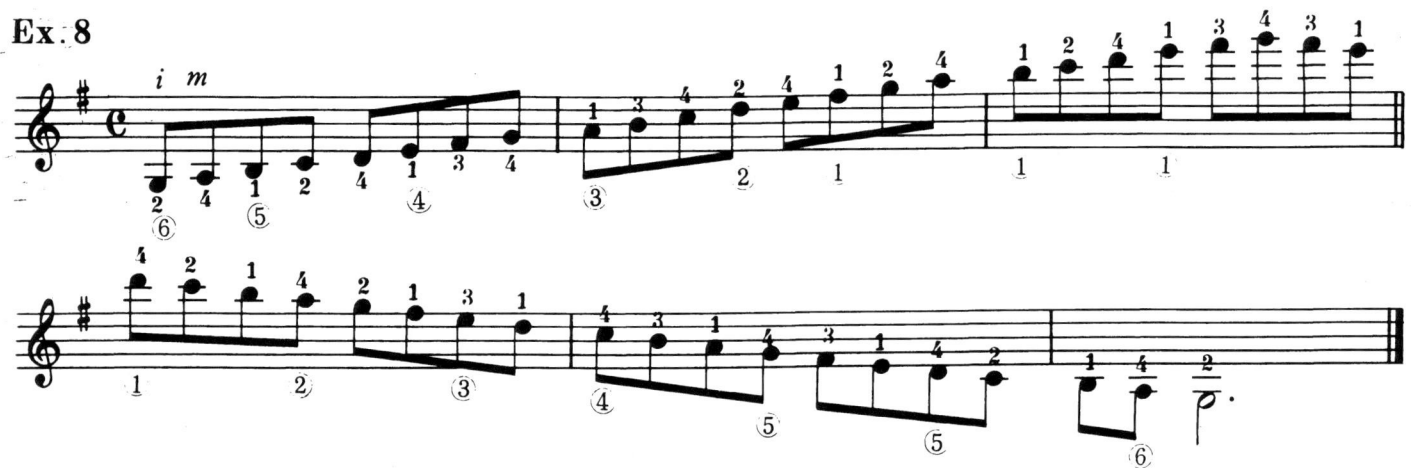

Ex. 9 Minor scale with first finger extension.

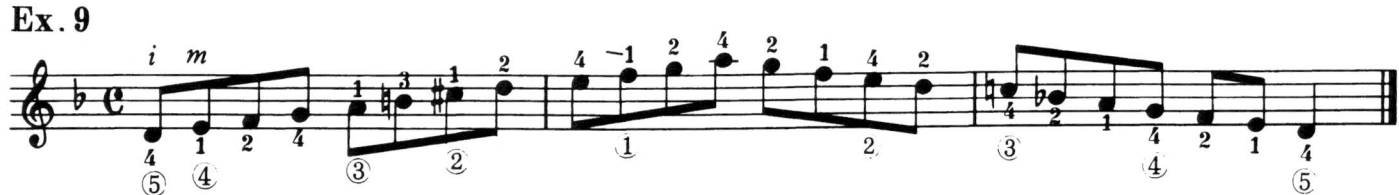

Ex. 10 Minor scale with first and fourth finger extensions.

Ex. 11 - 12 Minor scales requiring shifts.

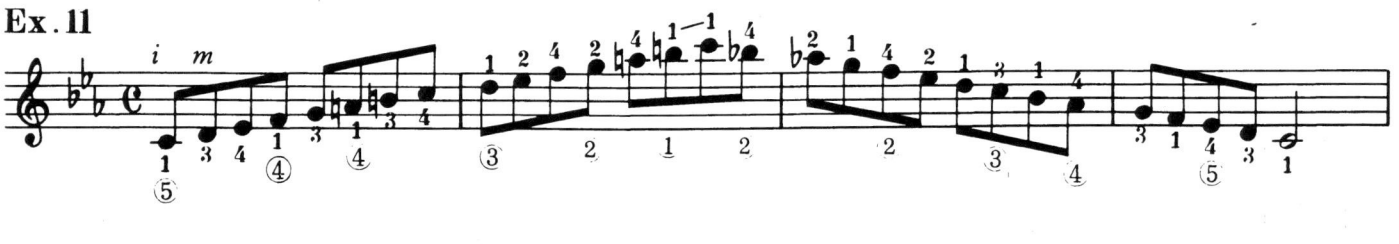

INTERVAL EXERCISES

Ex. 1 (a-f) Thirds with string crossings in the keys of C, G, D, A, E, and F. Some exercises require shifts.

Ex. 1

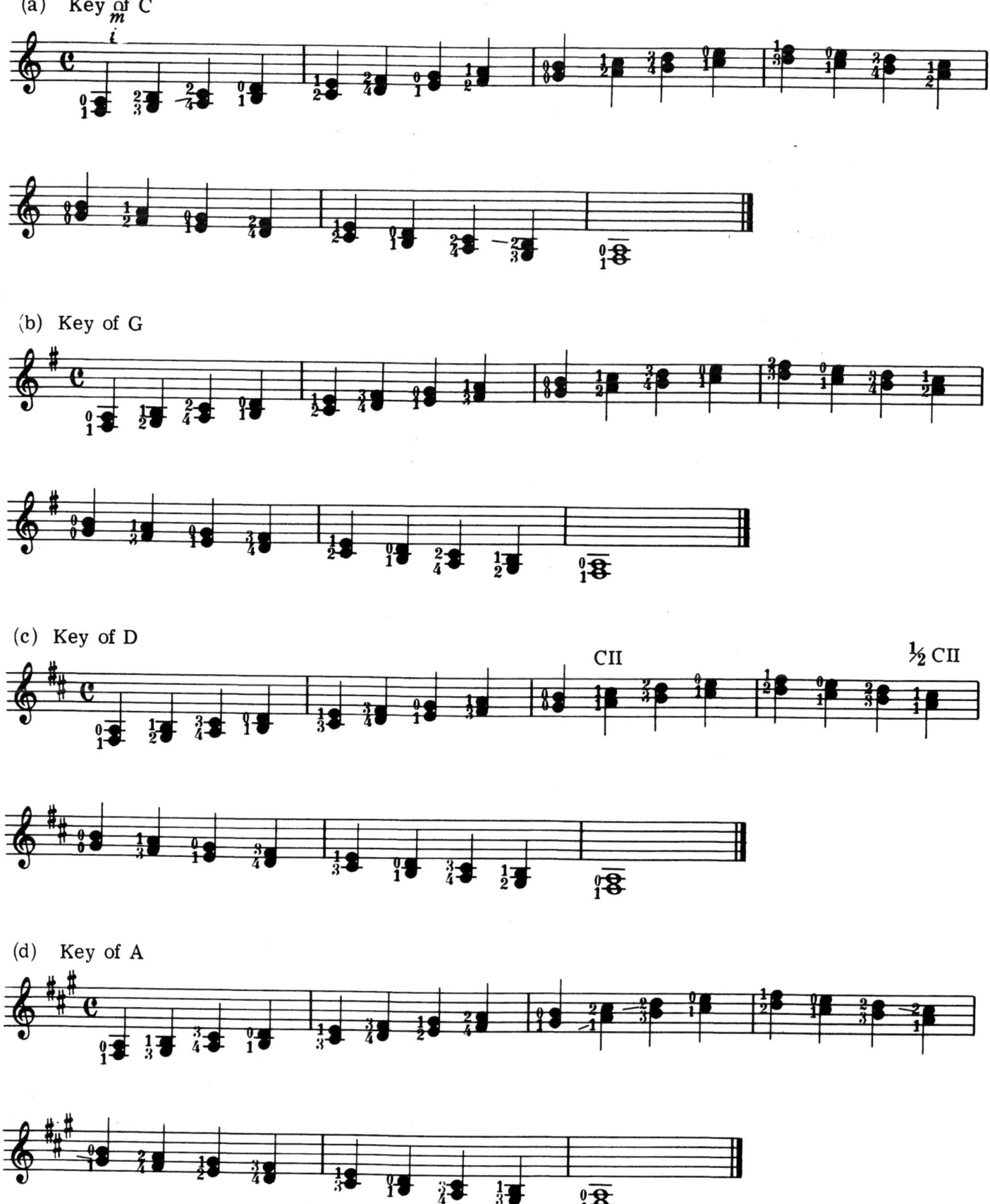

(e) Key of E

(f) Key of F

Ex. 2 (a-f) Sixths with string crossings in the same keys.

Ex. 2

(a) Key of C

(b) Key of G

(c) Key of D

(d) Key of A

(e) Key of E

(f) Key of F

Ex. 3 (a-f) Tenths with string crossings in the same keys.

Ex. 3

(a) Key of C

(b) Key of G

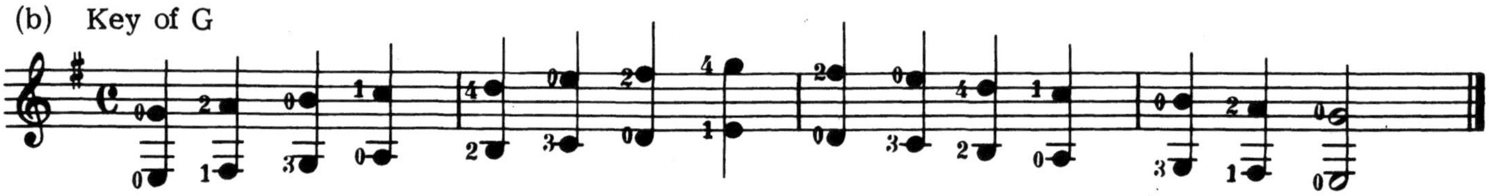

(c) Key of D

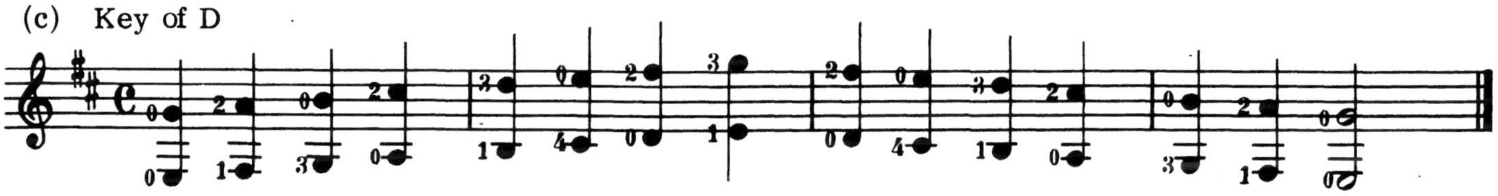

(d) Key of A

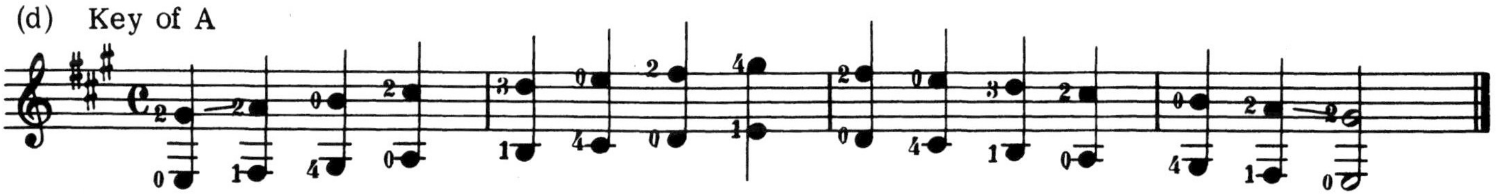

(e) Key of E

(f) Key of F

Ex. 4 (a-f) Thirds on strings ① and ② with shifts.

Ex. 4

(a) Key of C

m
i

(b) Key of G

(c) Key of D

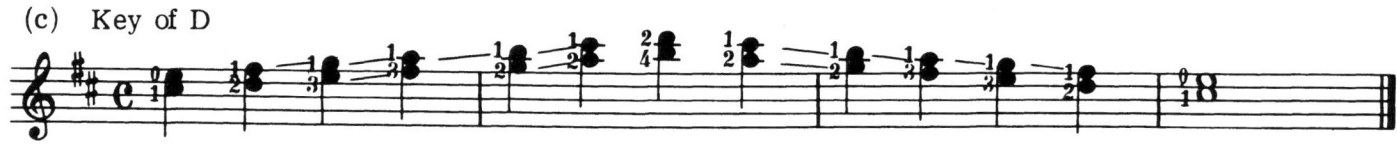

(d) Key of A

(e) Key of E

(f) Key of F

Ex. 5 (a-f) Thirds strings ② and ③ with shifts.

Ex.5

(a) Key of C

(b) Key of G

(c) Key of D

(d) Key of A

(e) Key of E

(f) Key of F

Ex. 6 (a-f) Sixths on strings ①and ③with shifts.

Ex. 6

(a) Key of C

(b) Key of G

(c) Key of D

(d) Key of A

(e) Key of E

(f) Key of F

Ex. 7 (a-f) Tenths on strings ①and ④with shifts.

Ex. 7

(a) Key of C

(b) Key of G

(c) Key of D

(d) Key of A

(e) Key of E

(f) Key of F

EXTENSION EXERCISES

Ex.1 - 4 In each exercise a finger must extend one fret higher or lower than normal. Be sure to keep the first note of each measure planted for the entire length of the measure. Each exercise should be played down to first position. Finger each note separately with the left hand. Do not use a barre.

Ex.1(c): measure 1. Beginning.

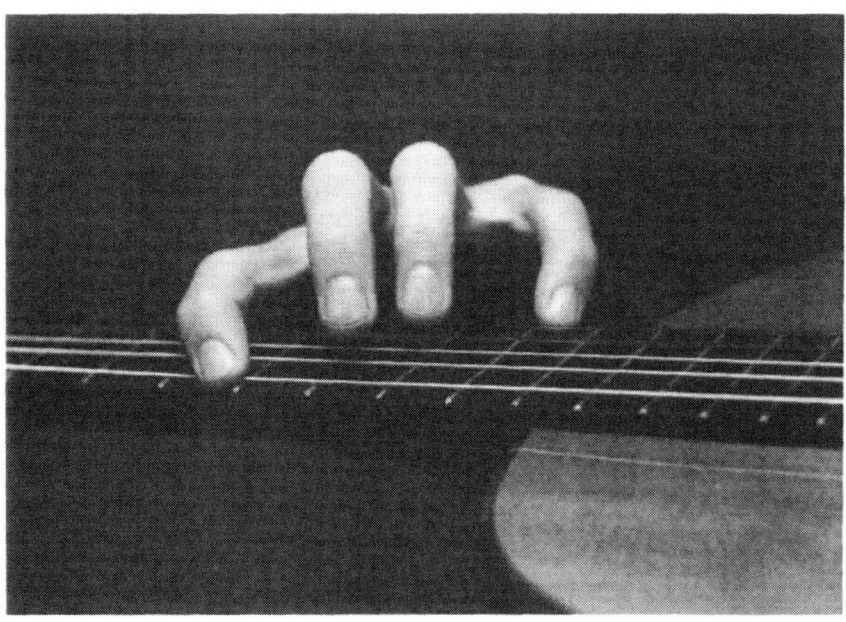

Ex.1(c): measure 1. End.

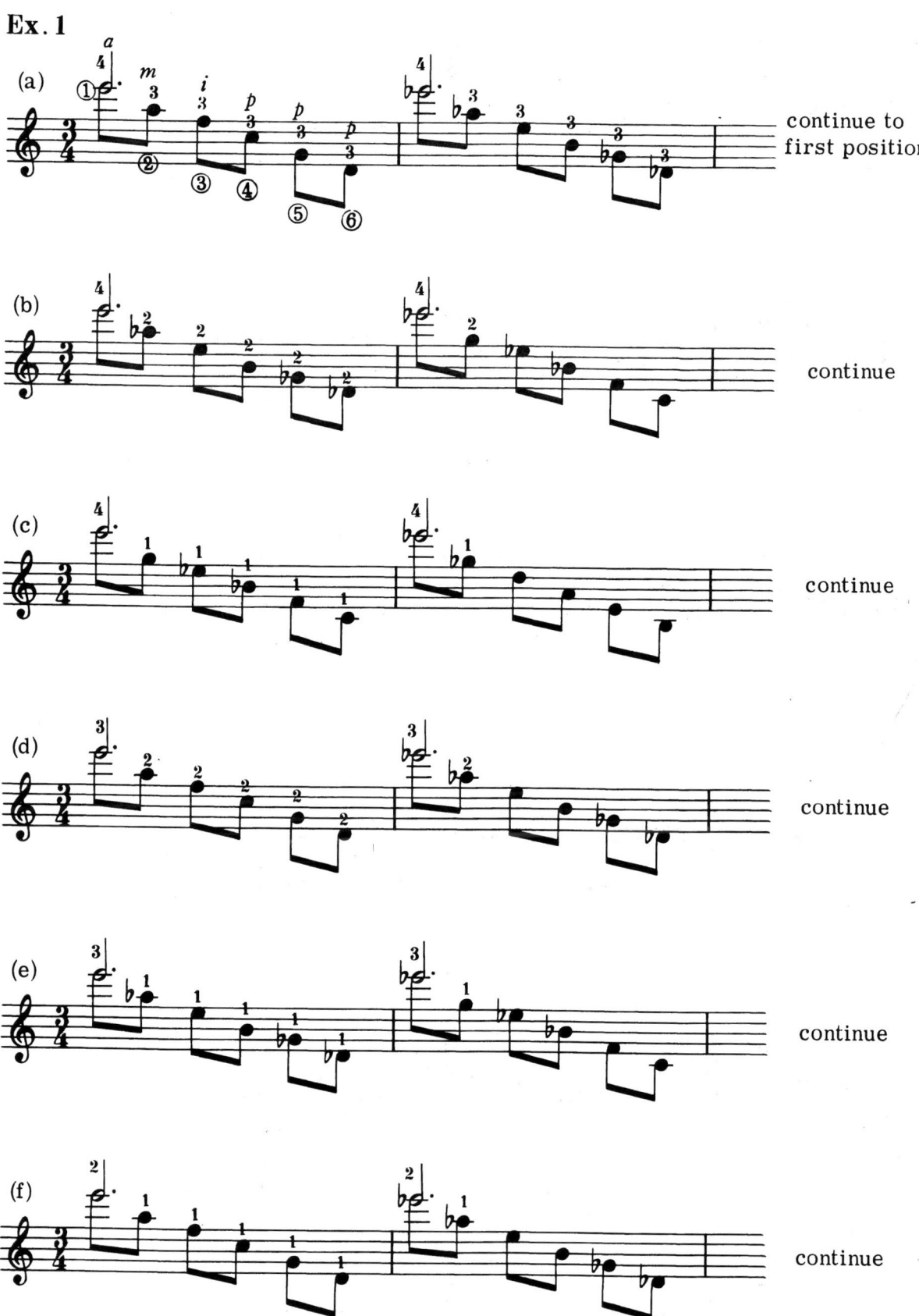

Ex. 2

(a)  continue

(b)  continue

(c)  continue

(d)  continue

(e)  continue

(f)  continue

Ex. 3

(a)

continue

(b)

continue

(c)

continue

(d)

continue

(d)

continue

(f)

continue

Ex. 4

(a)  continue

(b)  continue

(c)  continue

(d)  continue

(e)  continue

(f)  continue

Ex.5 (a-b) In each measure one finger must extend back one fret while the other fingers remain planted. (b) is the reversal and uses upward extensions.

continue until you reach first position

then reverse the pattern

continue until you reach ninth position

Ex.5(a): measure 1.

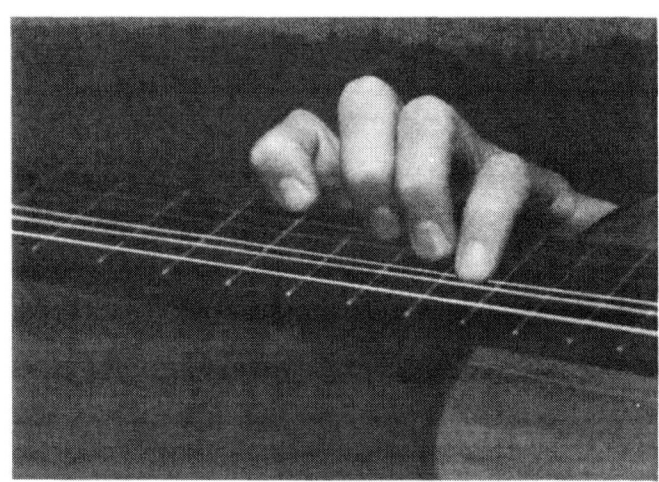

Measure 2.

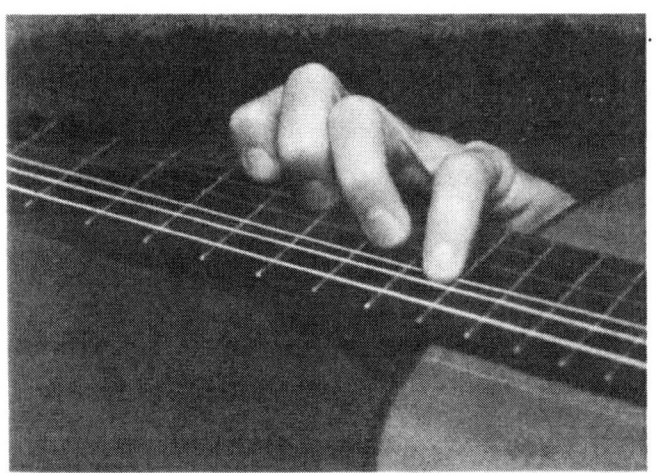

Measure 3.

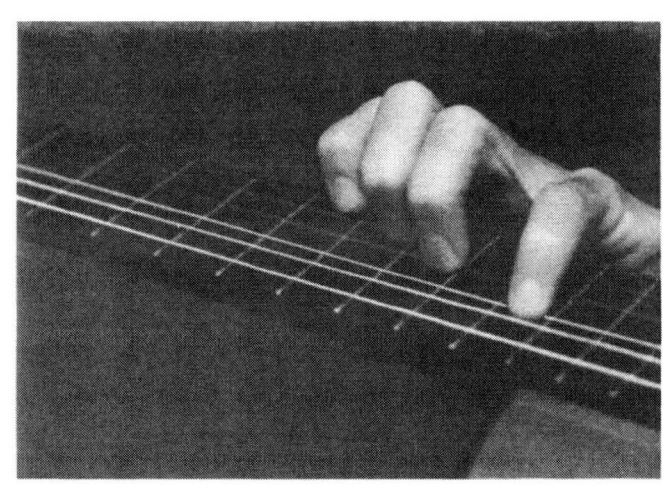

Measure 4.

Ex.6 (a-c) In (a) the fourth finger extends up one fret and back. In (b) the first finger extends down one fret and back. In (c) fingers one and four extend and return simultaneously. These patterns should be repeated one position lower until second position is reached.

Ex. 6

(a)

Repeat pattern one fret lower, etc.

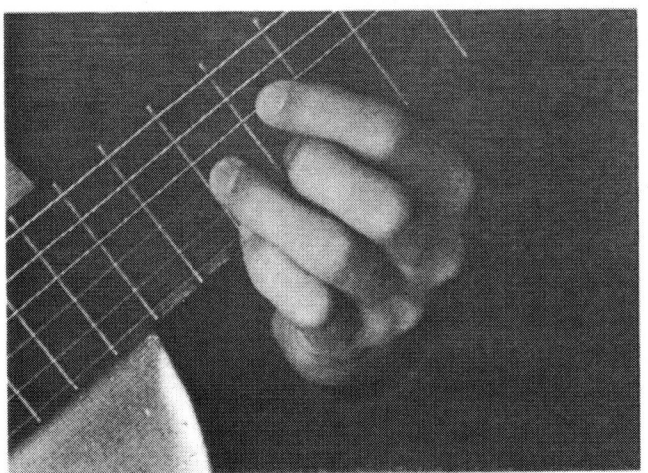

Ex.6(a): measure 1.

Measure 2.

(b)

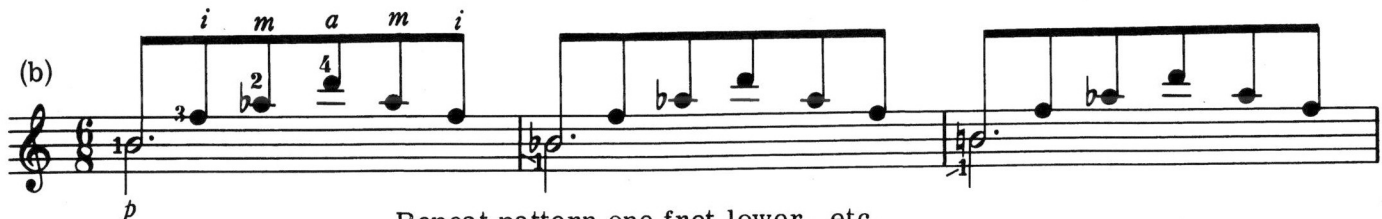

Repeat pattern one fret lower, etc.

Ex.6(b): measure 2.

(c)

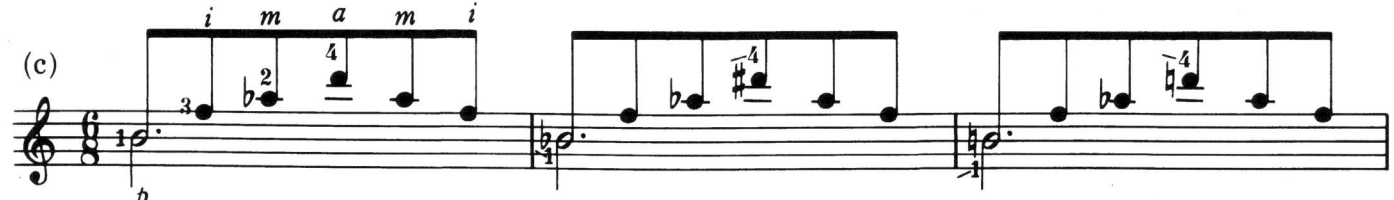

Repeat pattern one fret lower, etc.

Ex.6(c): measure 2.

Ex.7 (a-c) Same as Ex. 6 except that two fret extensions are required by both fingers.

Ex.7

(a)

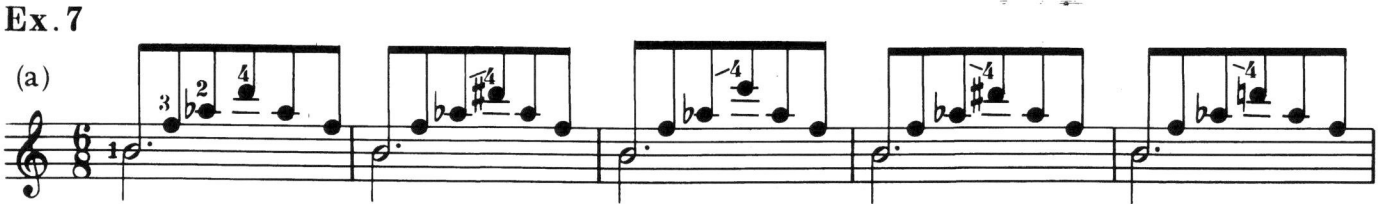

Repeat pattern one fret lower, etc.

(b)

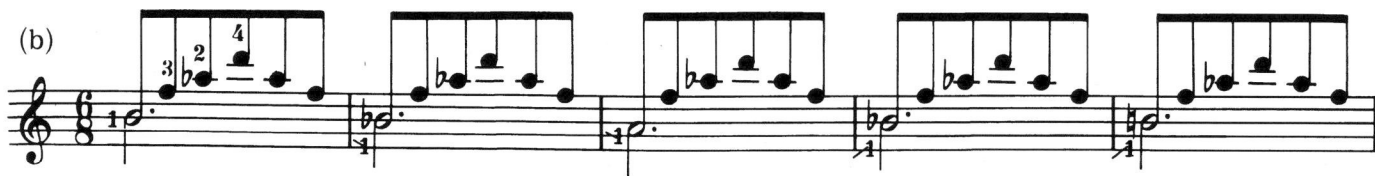

Repeat pattern one fret lower, etc.

(c)

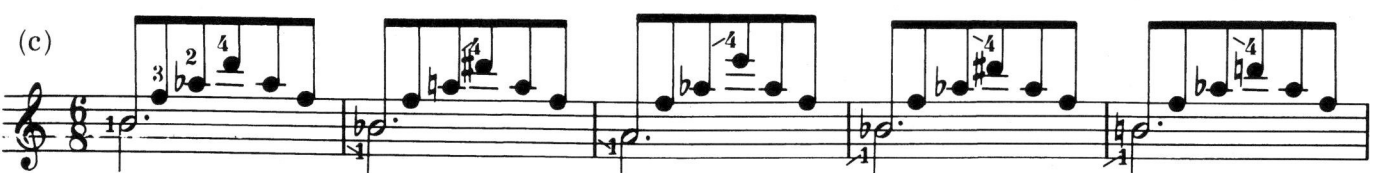

Ex.8 (a-c) Three extension studies. (b) and (c) follow the same harmonic progression as (a) but are written in a different key on different strings, making the extensions longer.

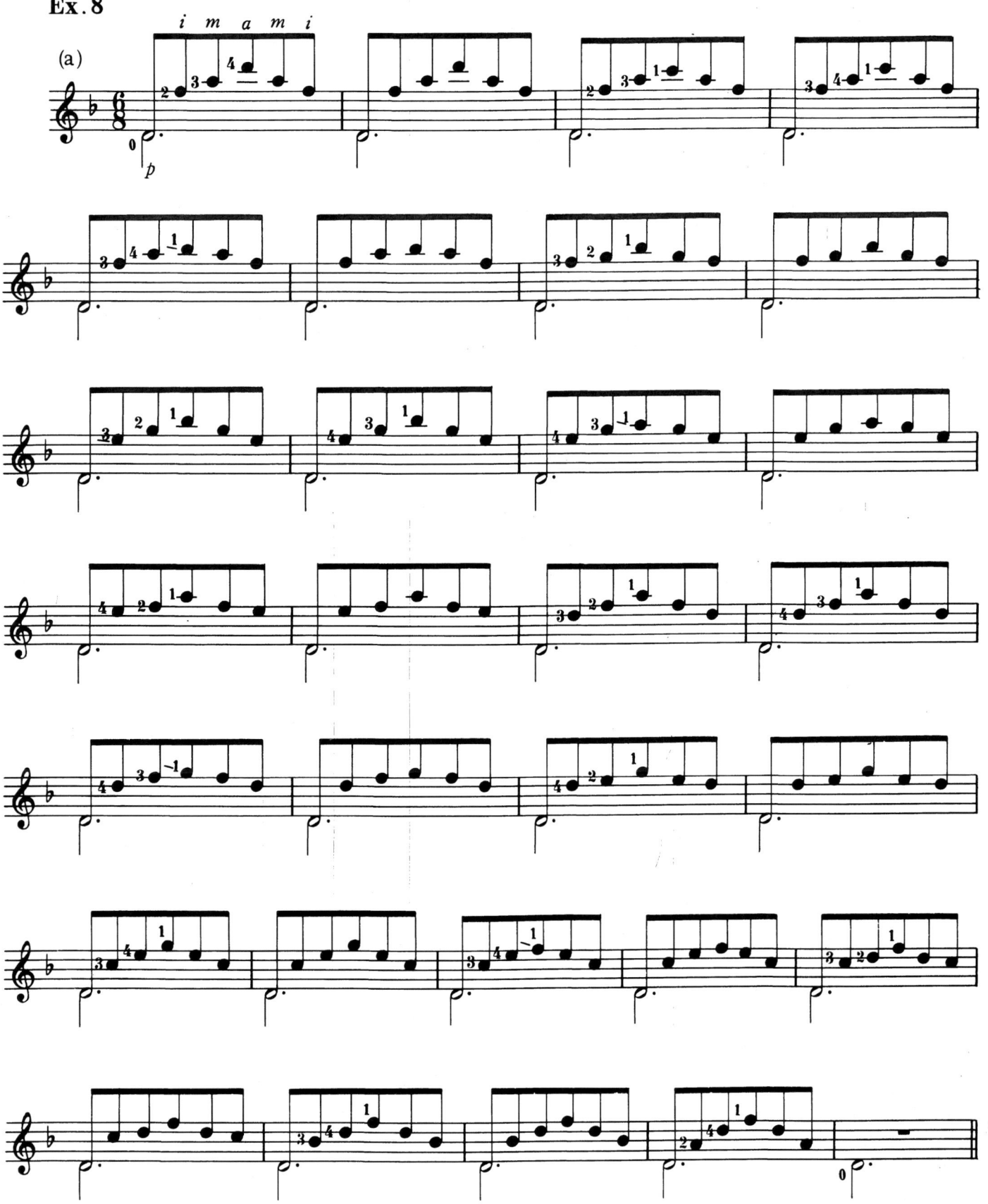

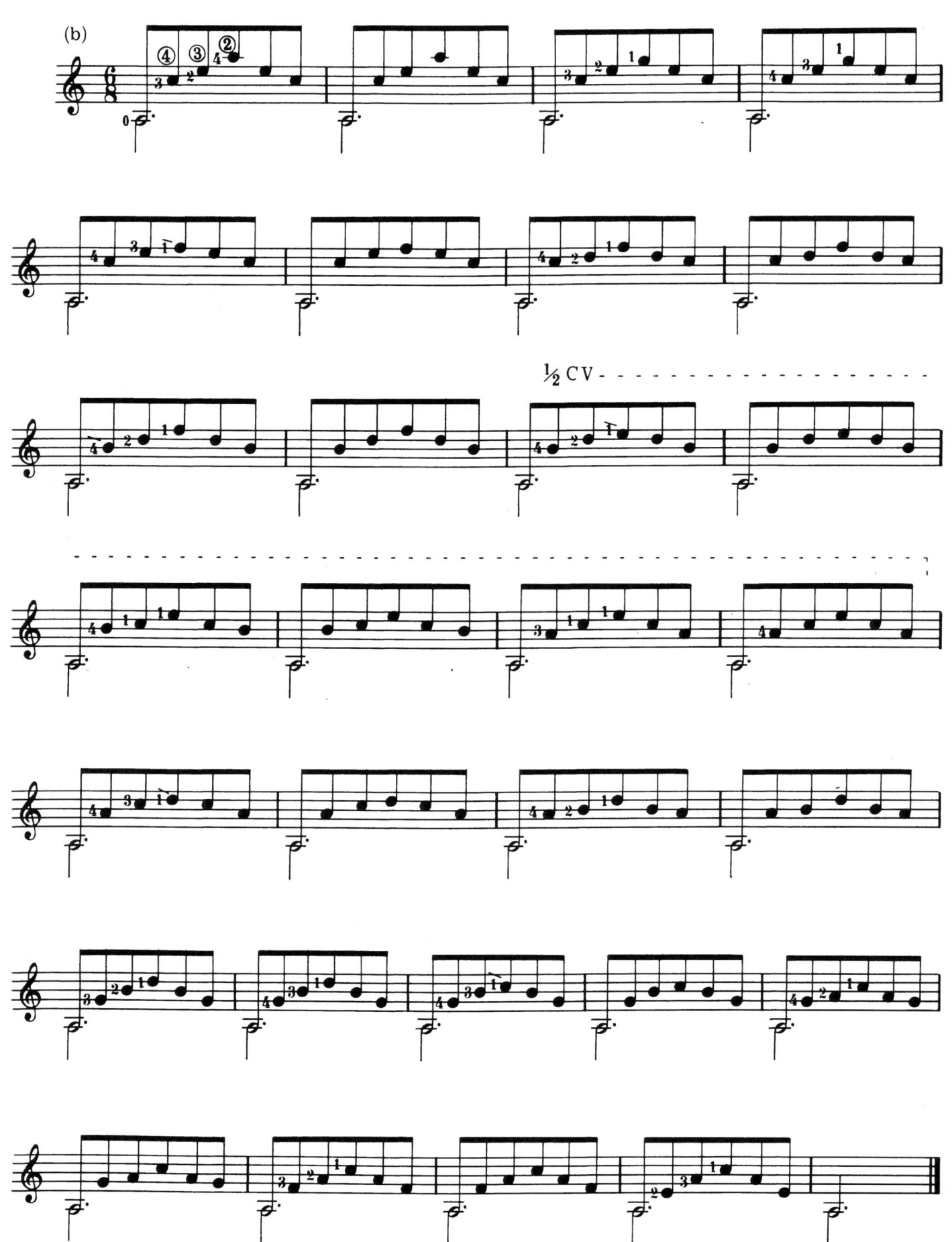

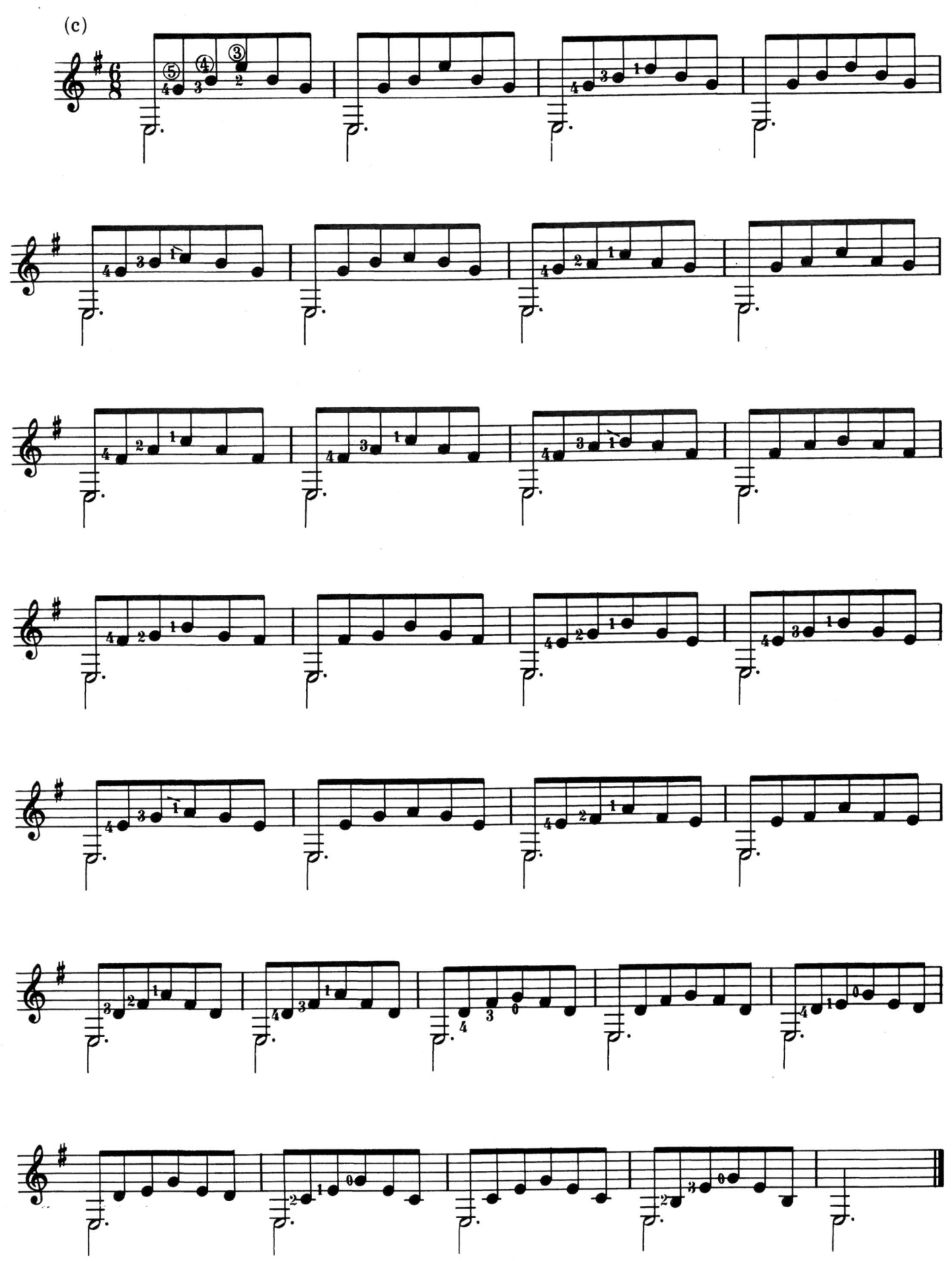

LEFT HAND HARMONIC EXERCISES

Left hand harmonics are produced by touching a string very accurately at specific points and then plucking the string with the right hand. Keep these ideas in mind when studying these exercises;

1. Do not press the string with the left hand; simply touch it at the proper spot.
2. Be sure to touch the string <u>exactly</u> in the required spot.

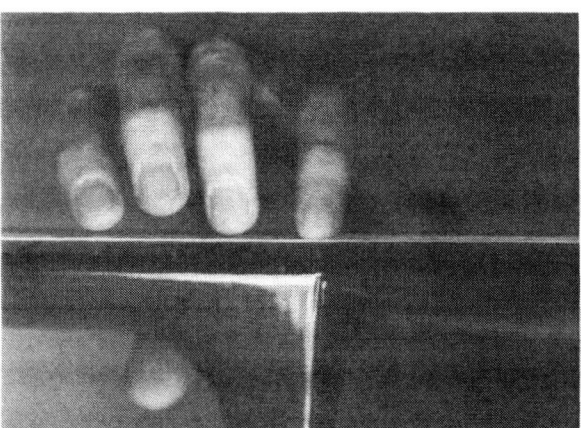

3. Take the finger off the string as soon as the harmonic is produced.

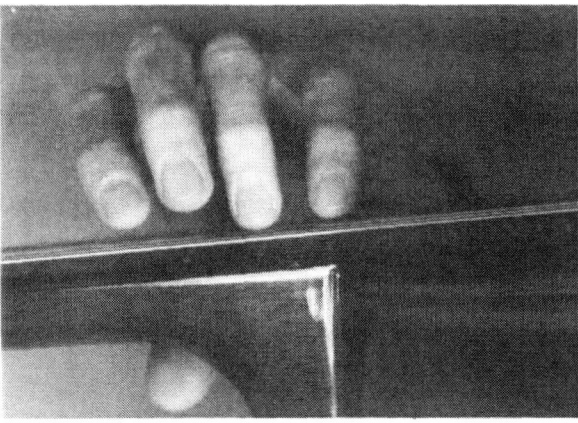

4. Be sure to pluck the strings close to the bridge with the right hand; otherwise many of the harmonics will not sound.

Ex.1 Harmonics at the twelfth fret. The string to be used is written as an open string. The number 12 indicates the fret at which the harmonic is found. Use the tip of the fourth finger to touch the string at a point directly above the twelfth fret. Move the finger to the different strings as necessary.

Ex. 1

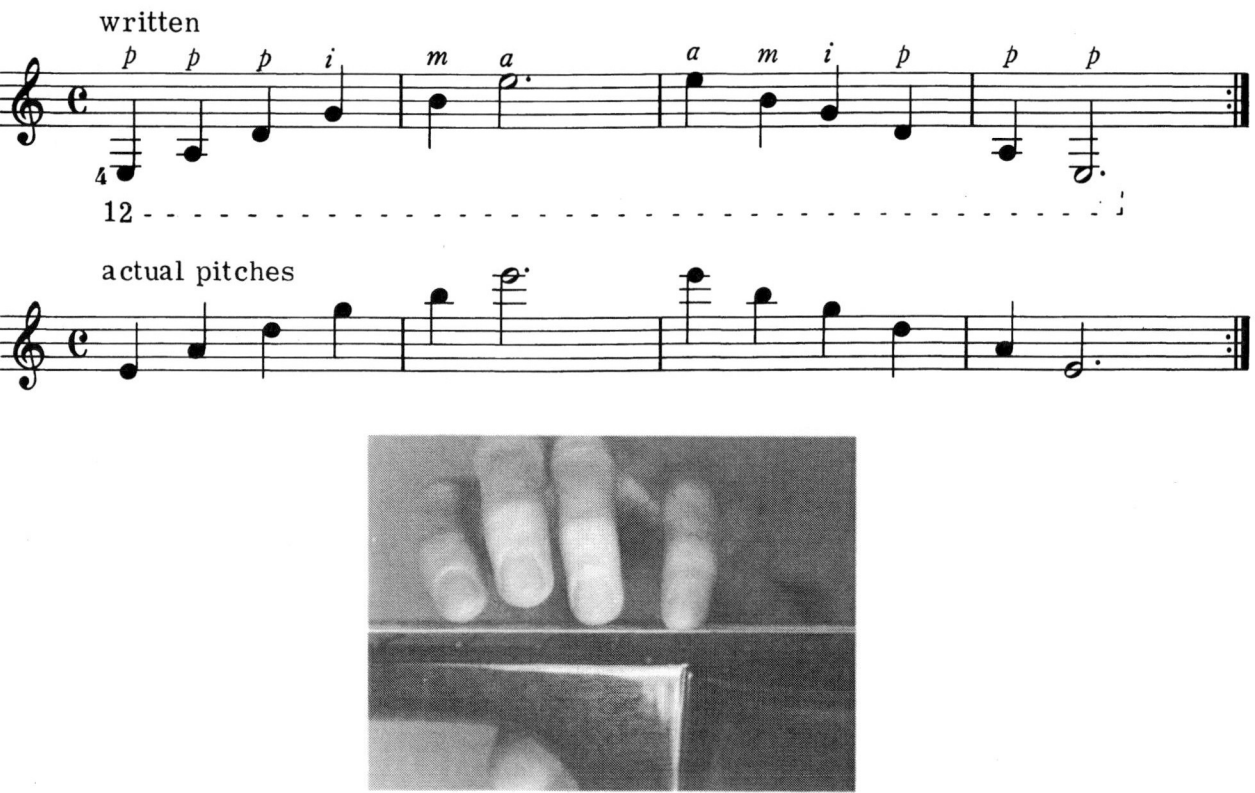

Ex.2 Harmonics at the seventh fret. Use the tip of the first finger. Also use fingers 2, 3, and 4.

Ex. 2

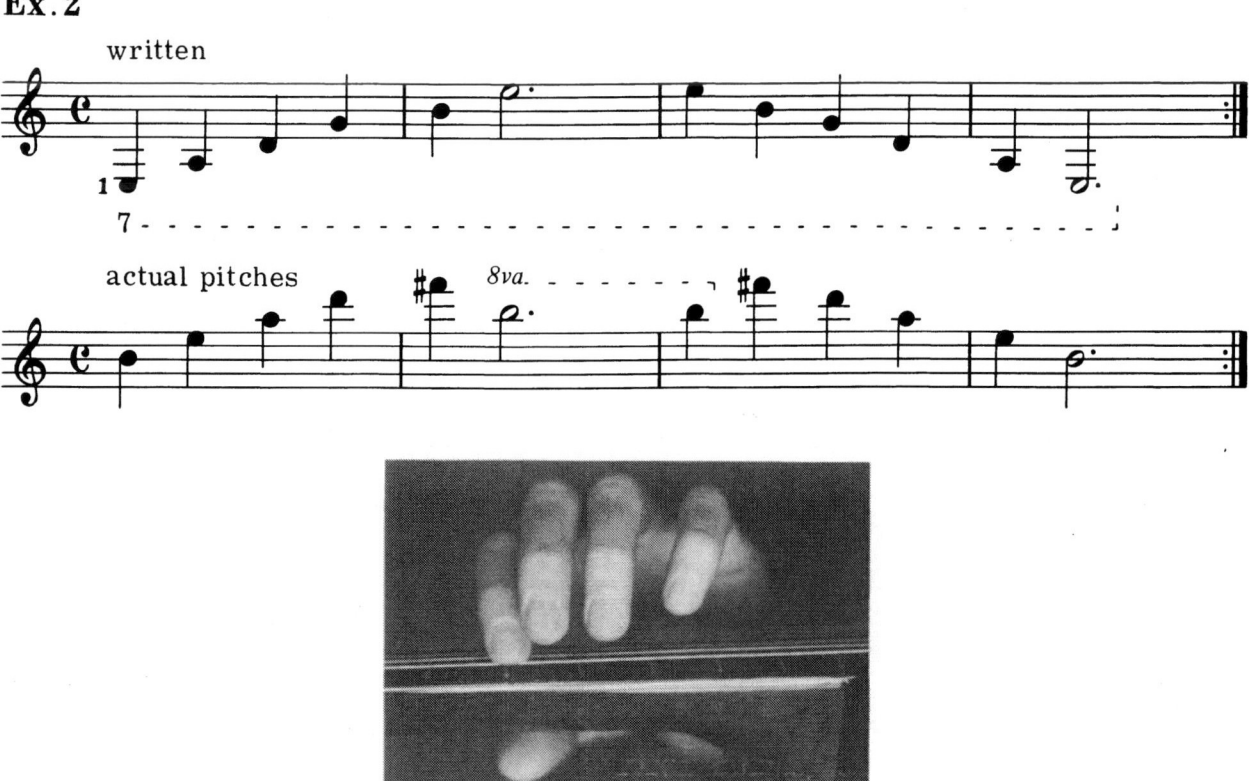

Ex.3 Harmonics at the fifth fret. Practice with all left hand fingers.

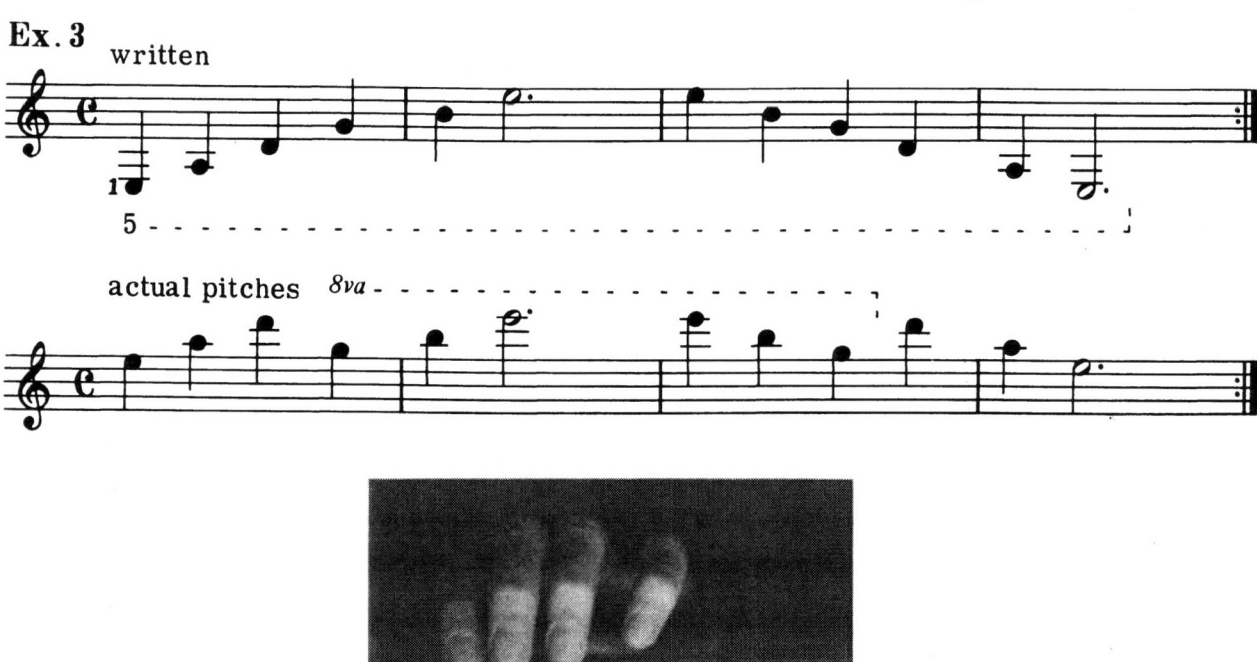

Ex.4 Harmonics at the fourth fret. These harmonics are found at a point just behind the fourth fret (towards the nut). Strings 4, 5, and 6 are the only strings commonly used for these harmonics.

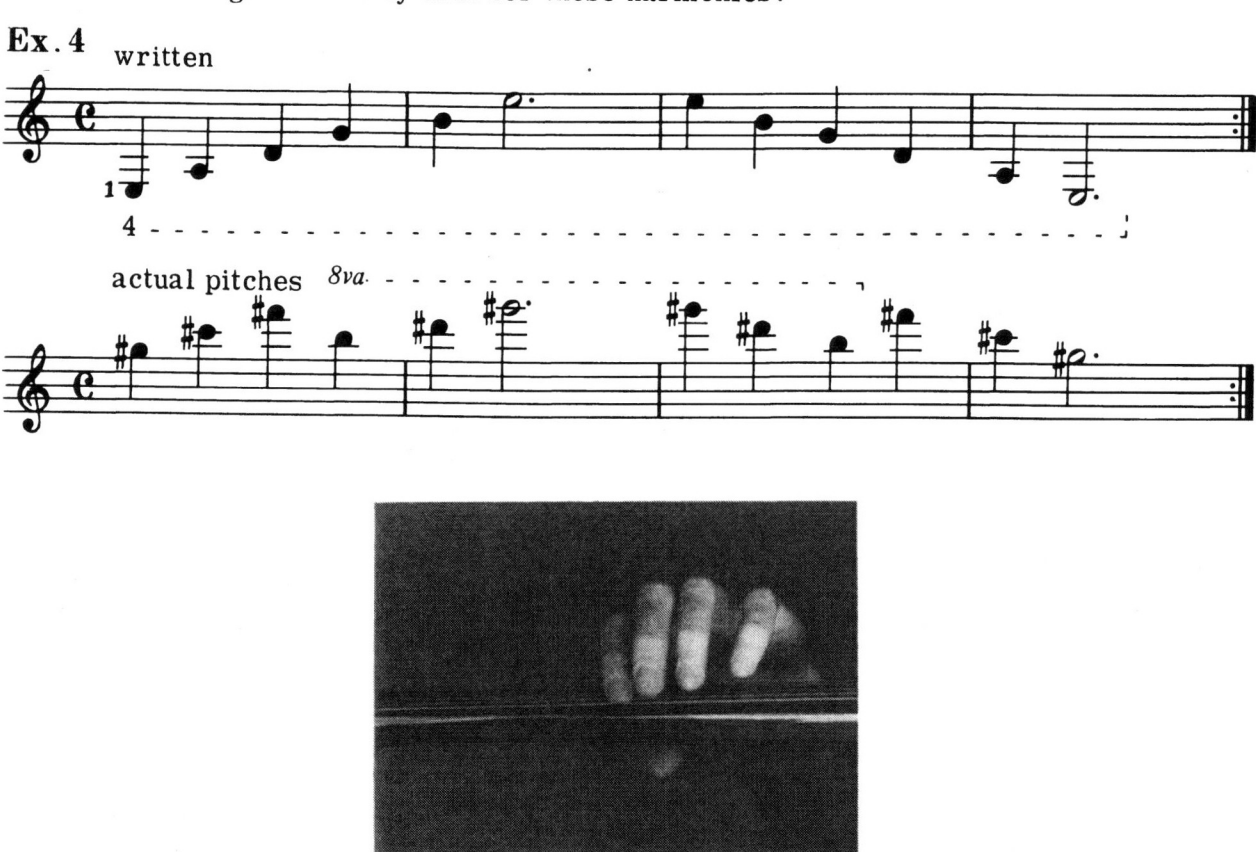

Ex.5 Harmonics at the third fret. These harmonics are found at a point just ahead of the third fret (towards the bridge). Strings 4, 5, and 6 are the only strings commonly used for these harmonics also.

Ex.5

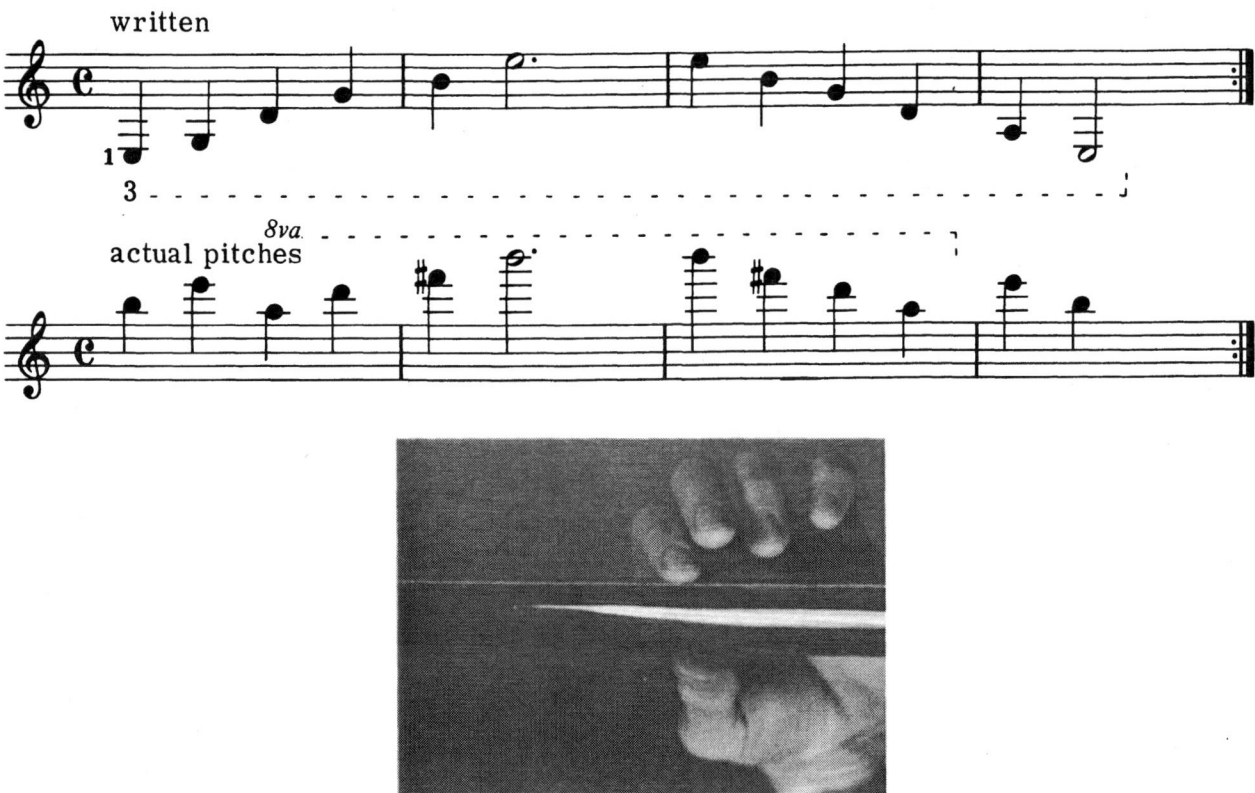

Ex.6 Harmonics at the ninth fret. These harmonics are found at a point just behind the ninth fret. They are identical in pitch to the fourth fret harmonics.

Ex.6

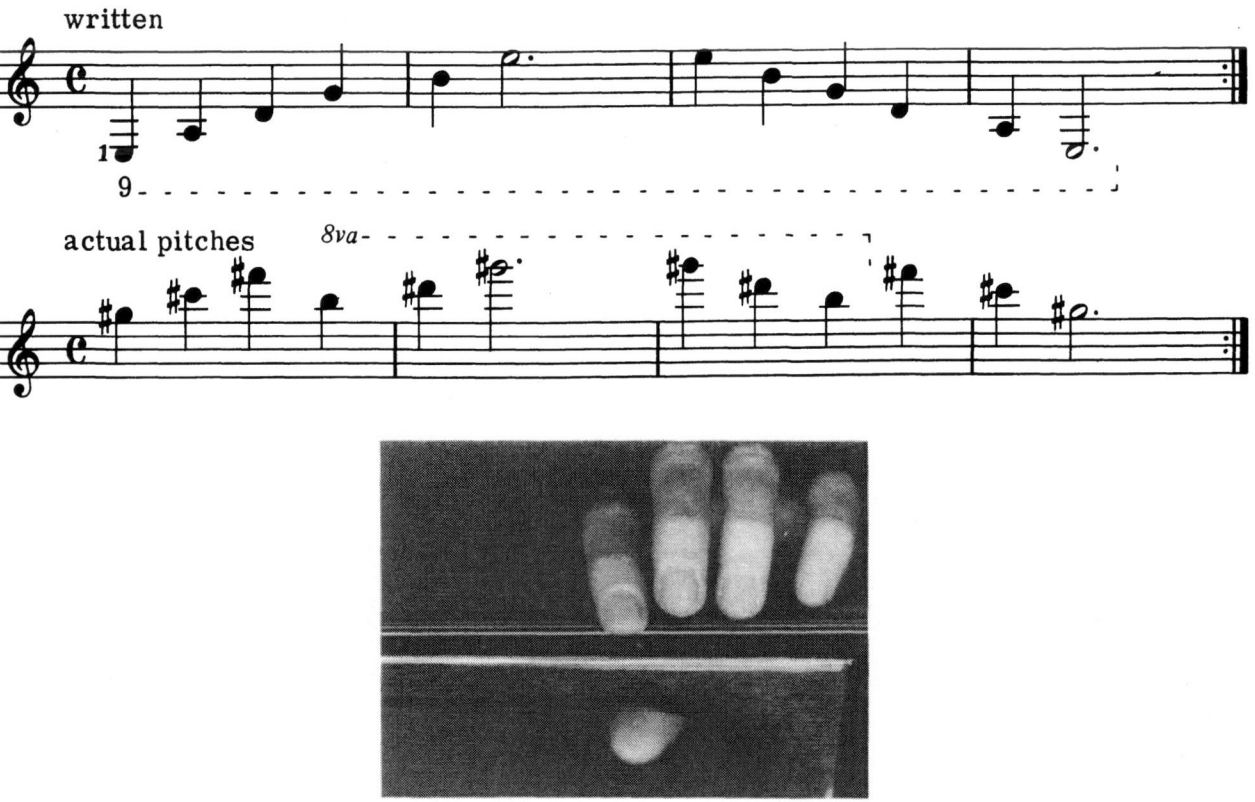

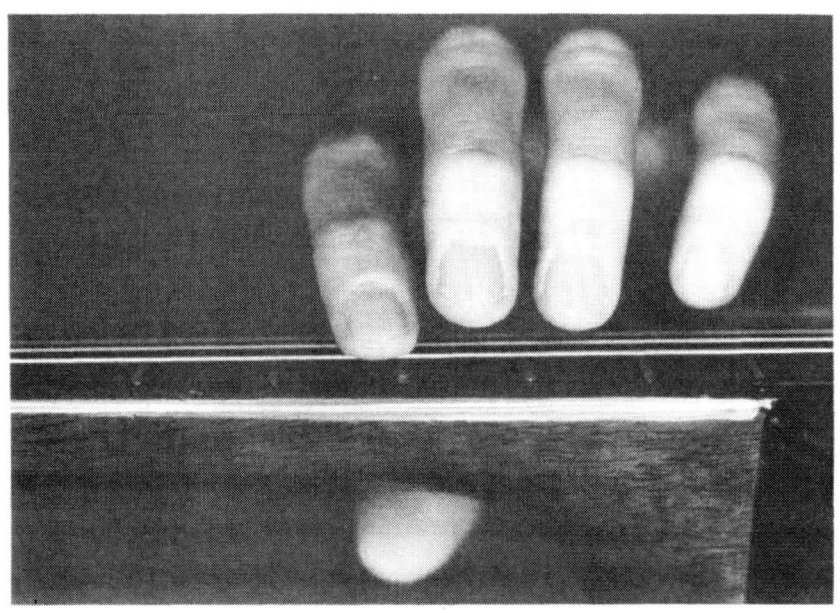

Ex.7 Progressive harmonics on one string. Practice on all strings.

Ex.7

Ex.8 - 9 Chords in harmonics. Be sure to get the first and fourth fingers exactly parallel to the frets. Use the entire tip segment of the finger to touch all three strings at once.

Ex.8

Ex.9

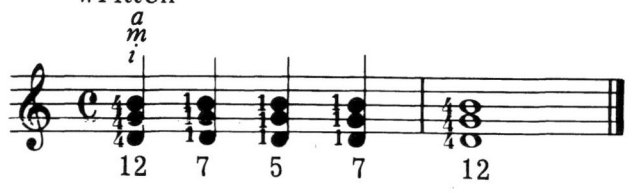

A NOTE ON THE STUDIES

These studies develop the skills presented in the previous exercises. Most of these studies involve chordal movement of the left hand. The chord changing and string crossing exercises are important in developing this technical area. In addition, look for these three circumstances in every chord change.

COMMON FINGER - Do the two chords have a note in common? If so, it is often played with the same finger.

GUIDE FINGER - The new chord may have a note or notes that are played on the same string with the same finger, but on a different fret than the old chord. This finger(s) can guide the hand to the new chord.

COMMON SHAPES - The new chord may contain a fingering pattern similar to the old chord, only the pattern is moved over one or more strings. Generally this will only occur with part of the chord i.e., two fingers will hold the same pattern but the other fingers do not. Occasionally the entire pattern will remain unchanged, simply moved to the new strings.

Look for these elements; they can make some chord changes much easier and faster to learn.

ANDANTINO

CHORDS	X	SCALES	
BARRES	⅚	INTERVALS	
SHIFTS		EXTENSIONS	
SLURS		HARMONICS	

F. Sor Op. 35 No. 18

48

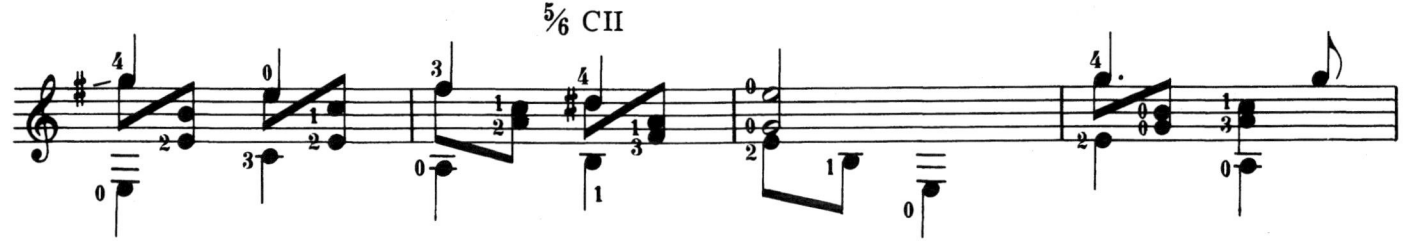

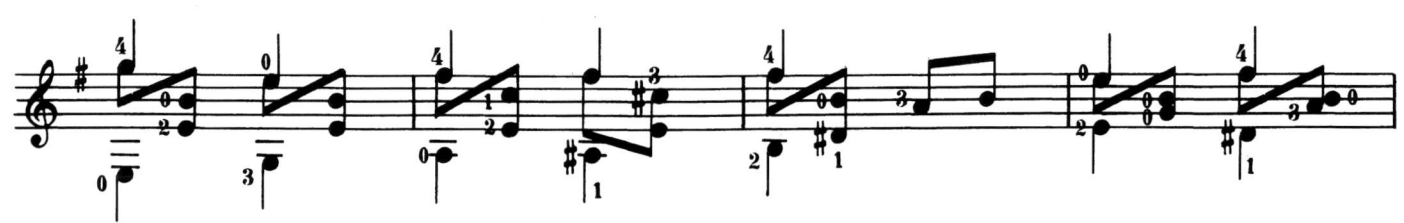

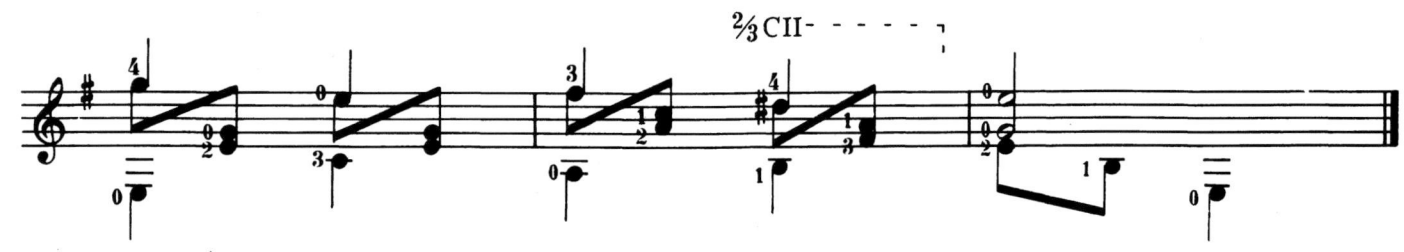

GRAZIOSO

ALLEGRO

CHORDS	X	SCALES	
BARRES	⅓ ½ full	INTERVALS	
SHIFTS		EXTENSIONS	
SLURS		HARMONICS	

M. Giuliani Op. 100 No. 22

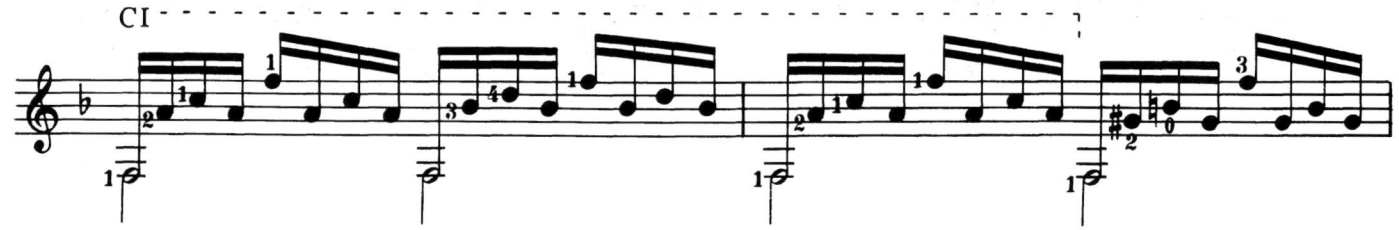

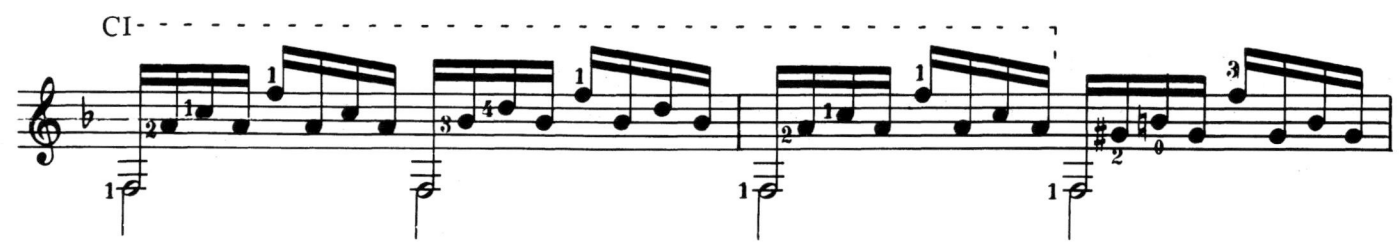

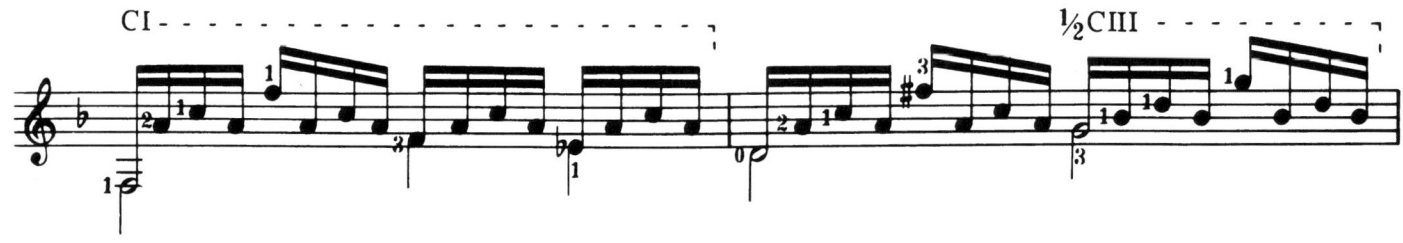

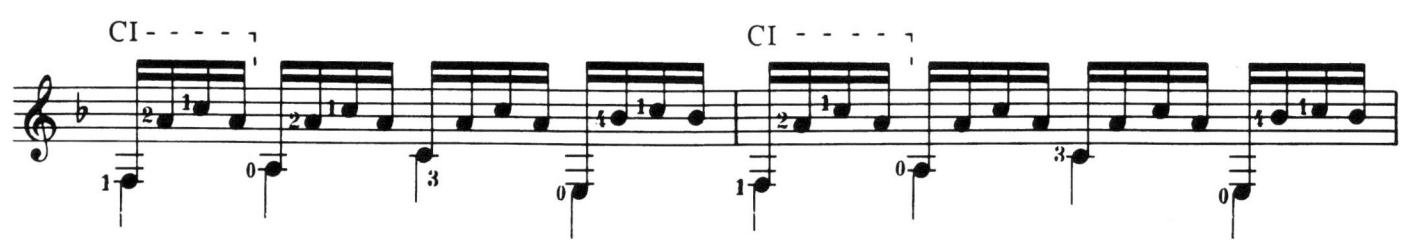

PRELUDE

CHORDS	X	SCALES	
BARRES	⅓ ½ ⅔ ⅚ full	INTERVALS	
SHIFTS	X	EXTENSIONS	
SLURS		HARMONICS	

F. Tarrega

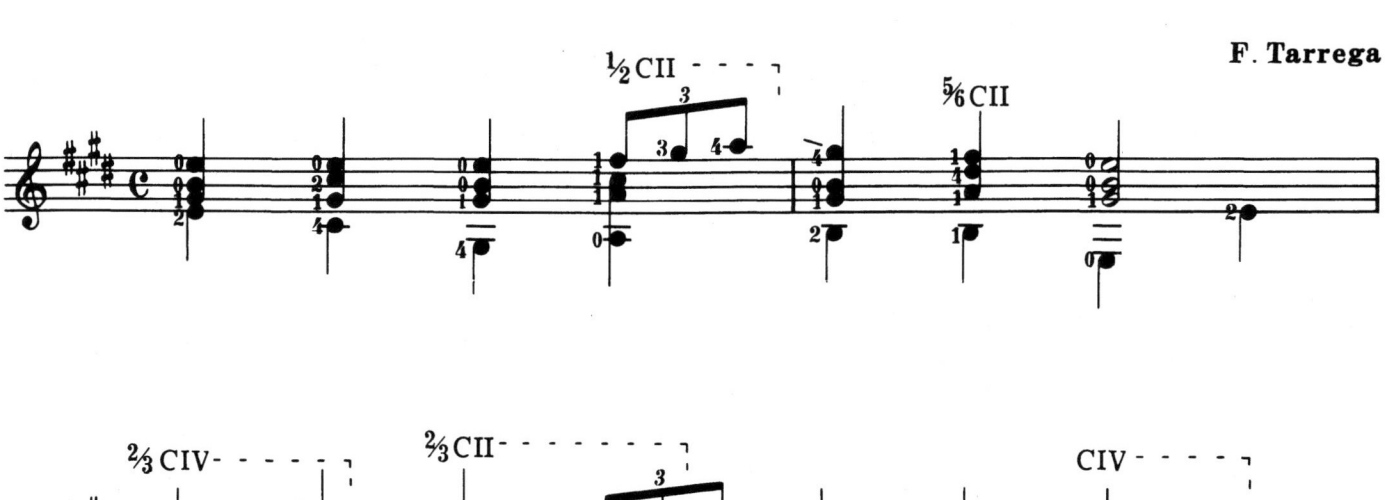

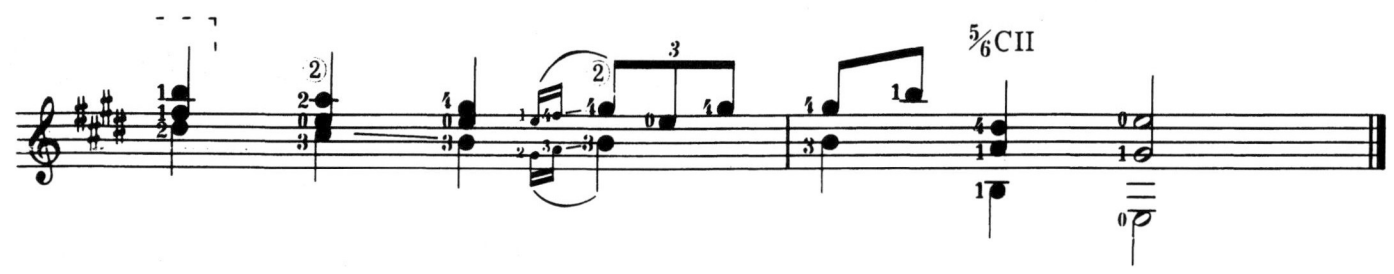

GRAZIOSO

CHORDS	X	SCALES	
BARRES	½ ⅔ ⅚ full	INTERVALS	
SHIFTS	X	EXTENSIONS	
SLURS		HARMONICS	

M. Giuliani Op. 100 No. 8

ANDANTINO

CHORDS	X	SCALES	
BARRES	½ ⅔ full	INTERVALS	
SHIFTS	X	EXTENSIONS	
SLURS		HARMONICS	

M. Giuliani Op. 100 No. 5

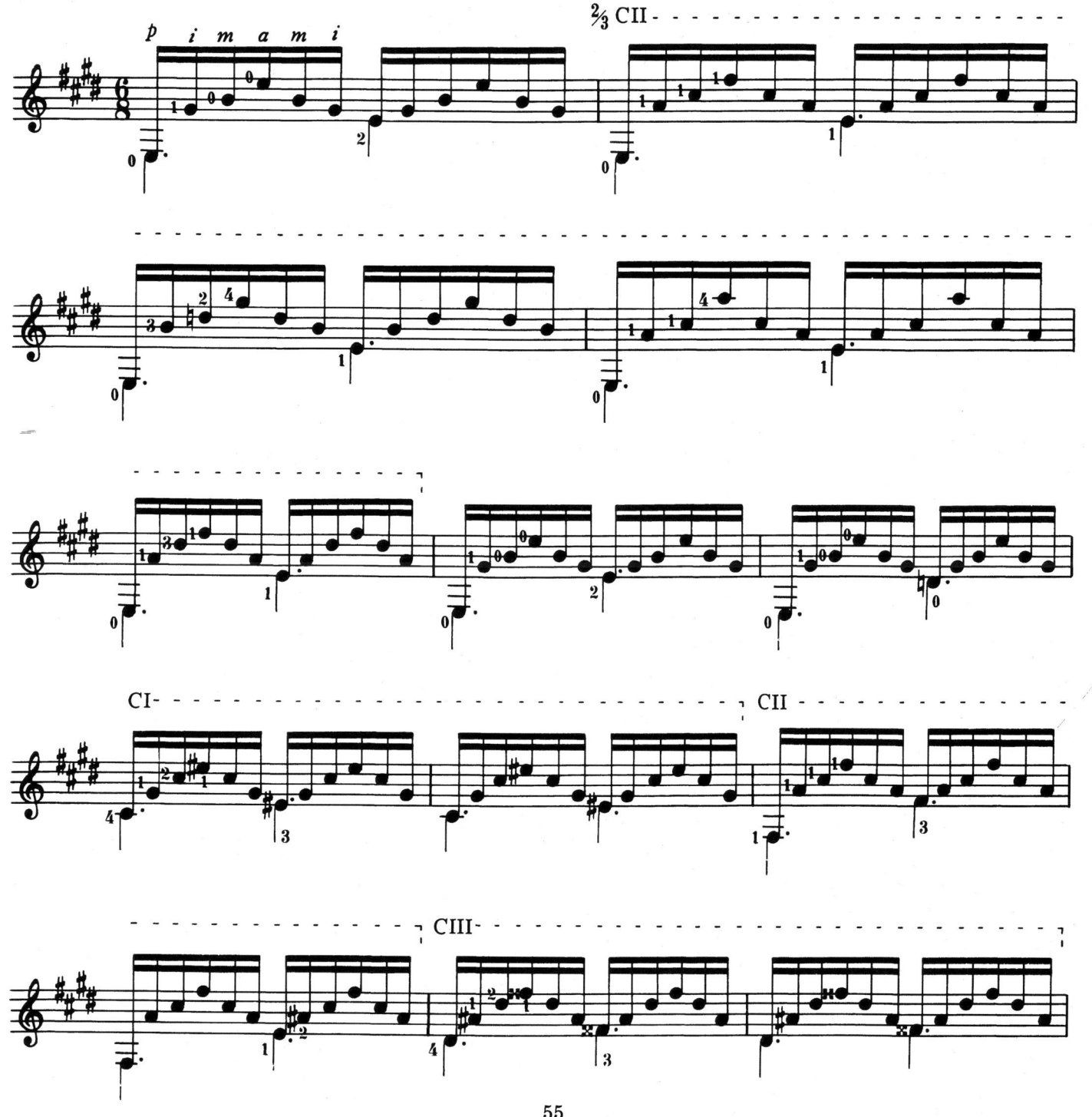

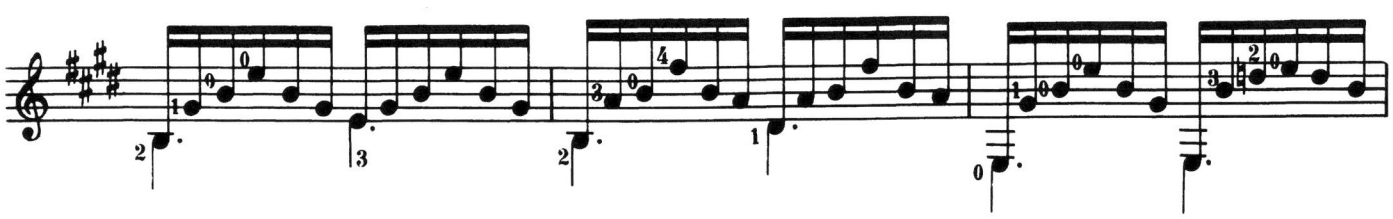
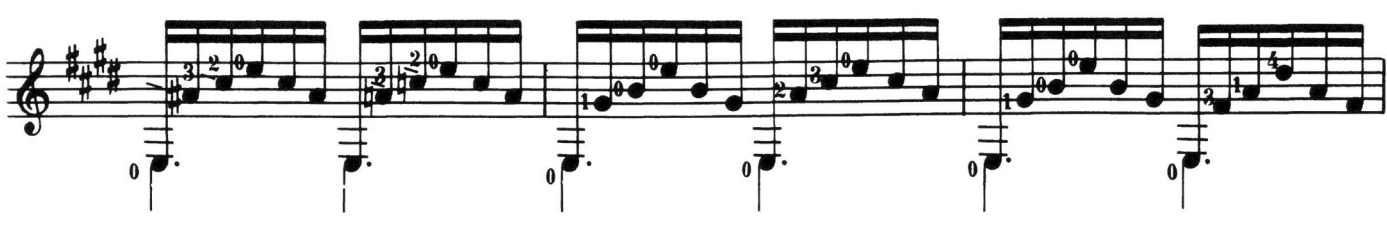

MODERATO

CHORDS	X	SCALES	
BARRES	⅓ ½ ⅔	INTERVALS	
SHIFTS	X	EXTENSIONS	
SLURS		HARMONICS	

F. Sor Op. 25

MODERATO

CHORDS	X	SCALES	
BARRES	⅓ ½ ⅔ full	INTERVALS	
SHIFTS	X	EXTENSIONS	
SLURS		HARMONICS	

F. Carulli

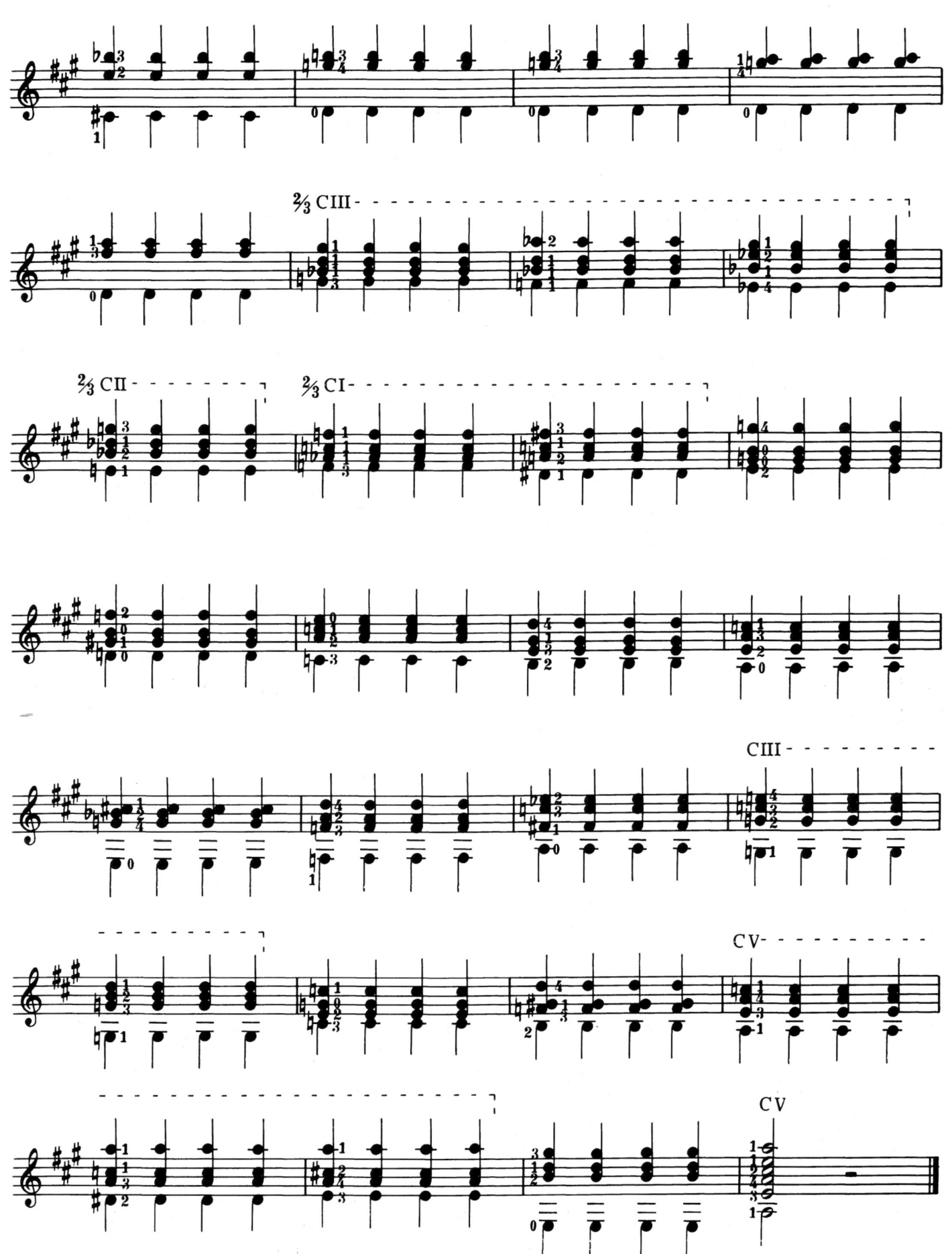

ANDANTE

CHORDS	X	SCALES	
BARRES	½ ⅔ ⅚ full	INTERVALS	
SHIFTS	X	EXTENSIONS	
SLURS		HARMONICS	

L. Beethoven
Trans. N. Coste

ANDANTE MOSSO

CHORDS	X	SCALES	
BARRES	½ ⅔	INTERVALS	
SHIFTS	X	EXTENSIONS	
SLURS		HARMONICS	

M. Carcassi Op. 60

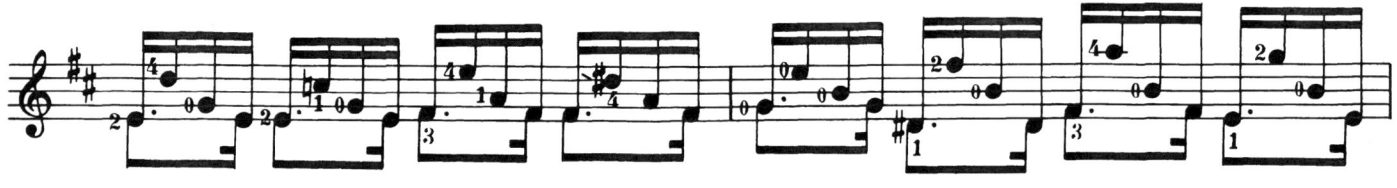

FOLIA DE ESPAÑA

CHORDS	X	SCALES	
BARRES		INTERVALS	
SHIFTS	X	EXTENSIONS	
SLURS		HARMONICS	

F. Tarrega

VIVACE

CHORDS	X	SCALES	
BARRES	1/3 1/2 2/3	INTERVALS	
SHIFTS	X	EXTENSIONS	
SLURS		HARMONICS	

M. Giuliani Op. 48

PRELUDE NO. 20

CHORDS	X	SCALES	
BARRES	⅔ ⅚ full	INTERVALS	
SHIFTS	X	EXTENSIONS	X
SLURS		HARMONICS	

F. Chopin
Trans. F. Tarrega

PRAYER

CHORDS	X	SCALES	
BARRES	½ ⅔ ⅚ full	INTERVALS	
SHIFTS	X	EXTENSIONS	
SLURS		HARMONICS	

F. Sor Op. 31 No. 22

SARABANDE

CHORDS	X	SCALES	
BARRES	⅓ ½ ⅔ ⅚	INTERVALS	
SHIFTS	X	EXTENSIONS	X
SLURS		HARMONICS	

J.S. Bach

BOURRÉE

CHORDS	X	SCALES	
BARRES	5/6 full	INTERVALS	
SHIFTS	X	EXTENSIONS	
SLURS		HARMONICS	

J.S. Bach

ANDANTINO

CHORDS		SCALES	
BARRES	⅔	INTERVALS	
SHIFTS		EXTENSIONS	
SLURS	X	HARMONICS	

M. Giuliani Op. 45

MODERATO

CHORDS		SCALES	
BARRES	½ ⅚	INTERVALS	
SHIFTS	X	EXTENSIONS	
SLURS	X	HARMONICS	

D. Aguado

DOLCE ESPRESSIVO

CHORDS		SCALES	
BARRES		INTERVALS	
SHIFTS	X	EXTENSIONS	
SLURS	X	HARMONICS	

M. Giuliani Op. 9

ANDANTE

CHORDS		SCALES	
BARRES	½	INTERVALS	
SHIFTS	X	EXTENSIONS	
SLURS	X	HARMONICS	

M. Carcassi Op. 7

LARGO

CHORDS		SCALES	
BARRES	full	INTERVALS	
SHIFTS	X	EXTENSIONS	
SLURS	X	HARMONICS	

F. Sor Op. 3

CANARIOS

CHORDS		SCALES	
BARRES		INTERVALS	
SHIFTS	X	EXTENSIONS	
SLURS	X	HARMONICS	

G. Sanz

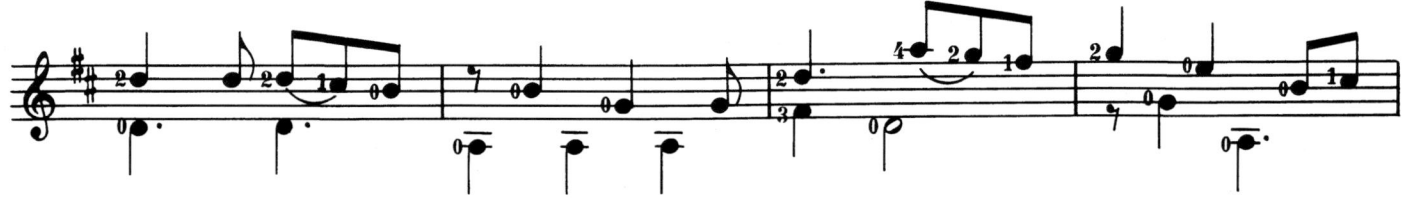

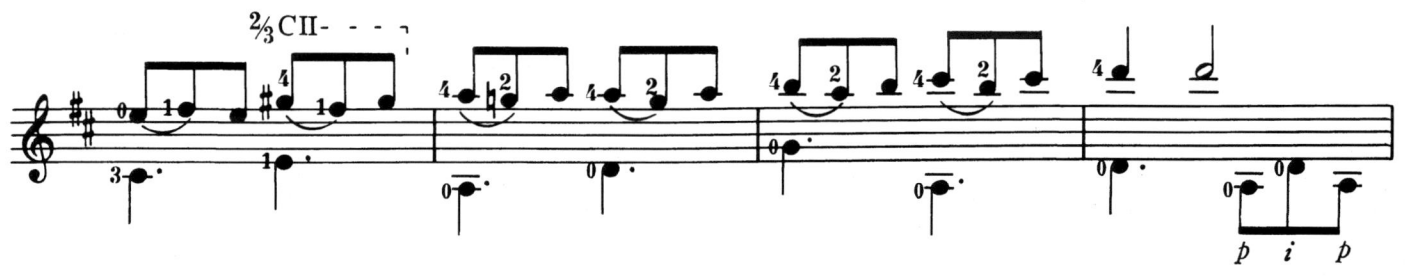

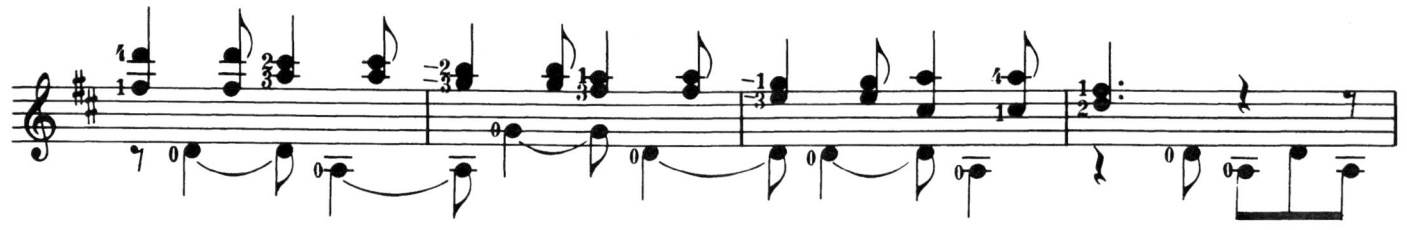

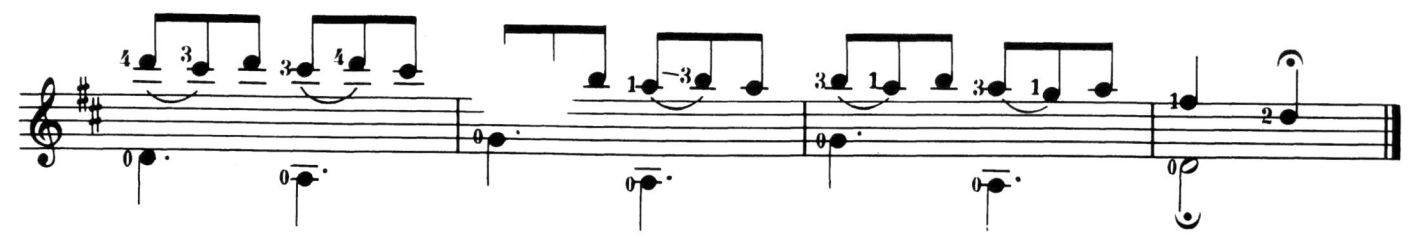

VALSE

CHORDS			SCALES	
BARRES	½	⅚	INTERVALS	X
SHIFTS	X		EXTENSIONS	
SLURS	X		HARMONICS	

F. Sor Op. 23

STUDY

CHORDS	X	SCALES	
BARRES	⅓ ½ ⅚ full	INTERVALS	
SHIFTS	X	EXTENSIONS	
SLURS	X	HARMONICS	

F. Tarrega

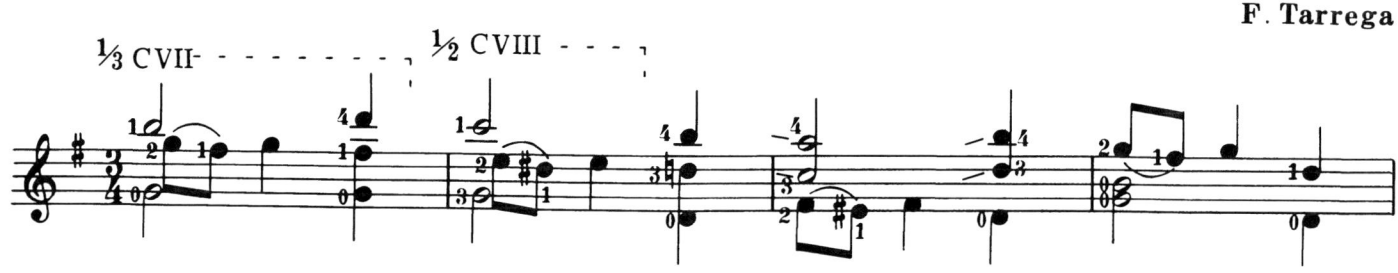

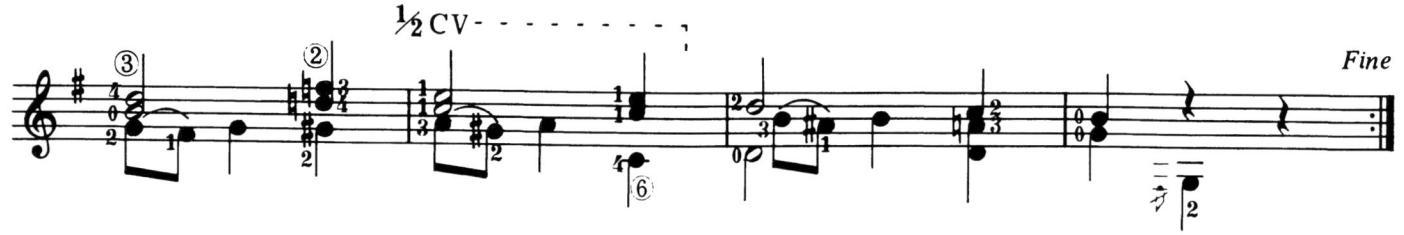

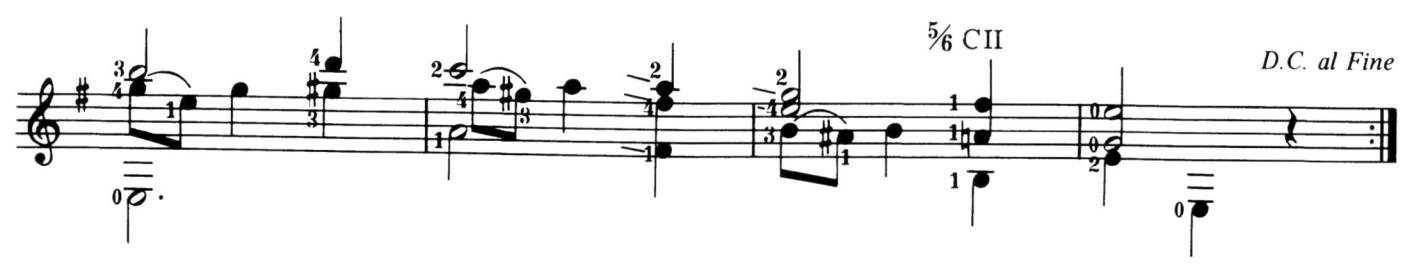

ALLEGRO

CHORDS	X	SCALES	X
BARRES	⅓	INTERVALS	
SHIFTS	X	EXTENSIONS	
SLURS		HARMONICS	

M. Carcassi Op. 60

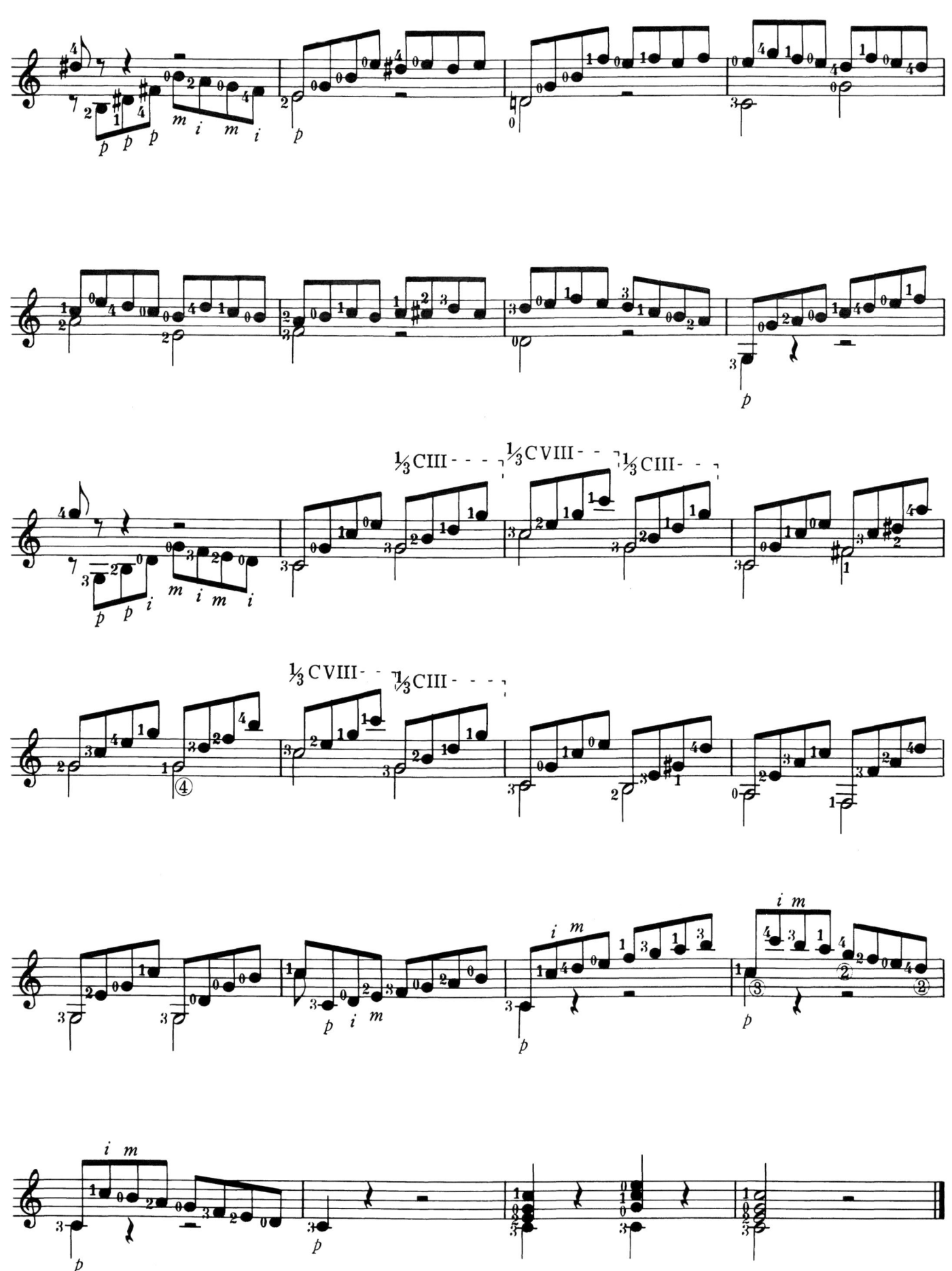

ALLEGRETTO

CHORDS		SCALES	X
BARRES	⅓ ½ ⅚ full	INTERVALS	
SHIFTS	X	EXTENSIONS	X
SLURS		HARMONICS	

M. Carcassi Op. 60

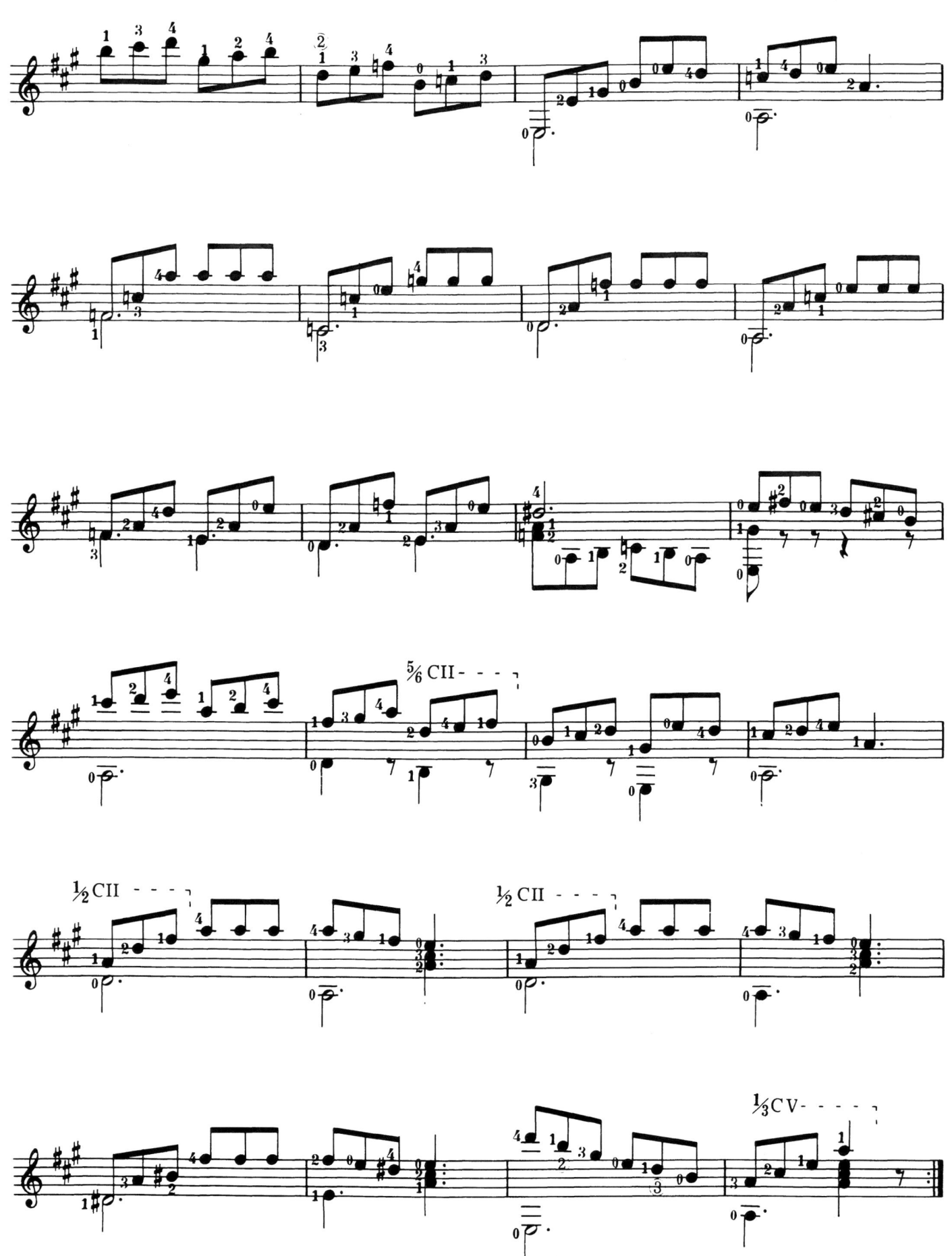

ALLEGRO

CHORDS		SCALES	X
BARRES	½ ⅔ full	INTERVALS	
SHIFTS	X	EXTENSIONS	
SLURS		HARMONICS	

F. Tarrega

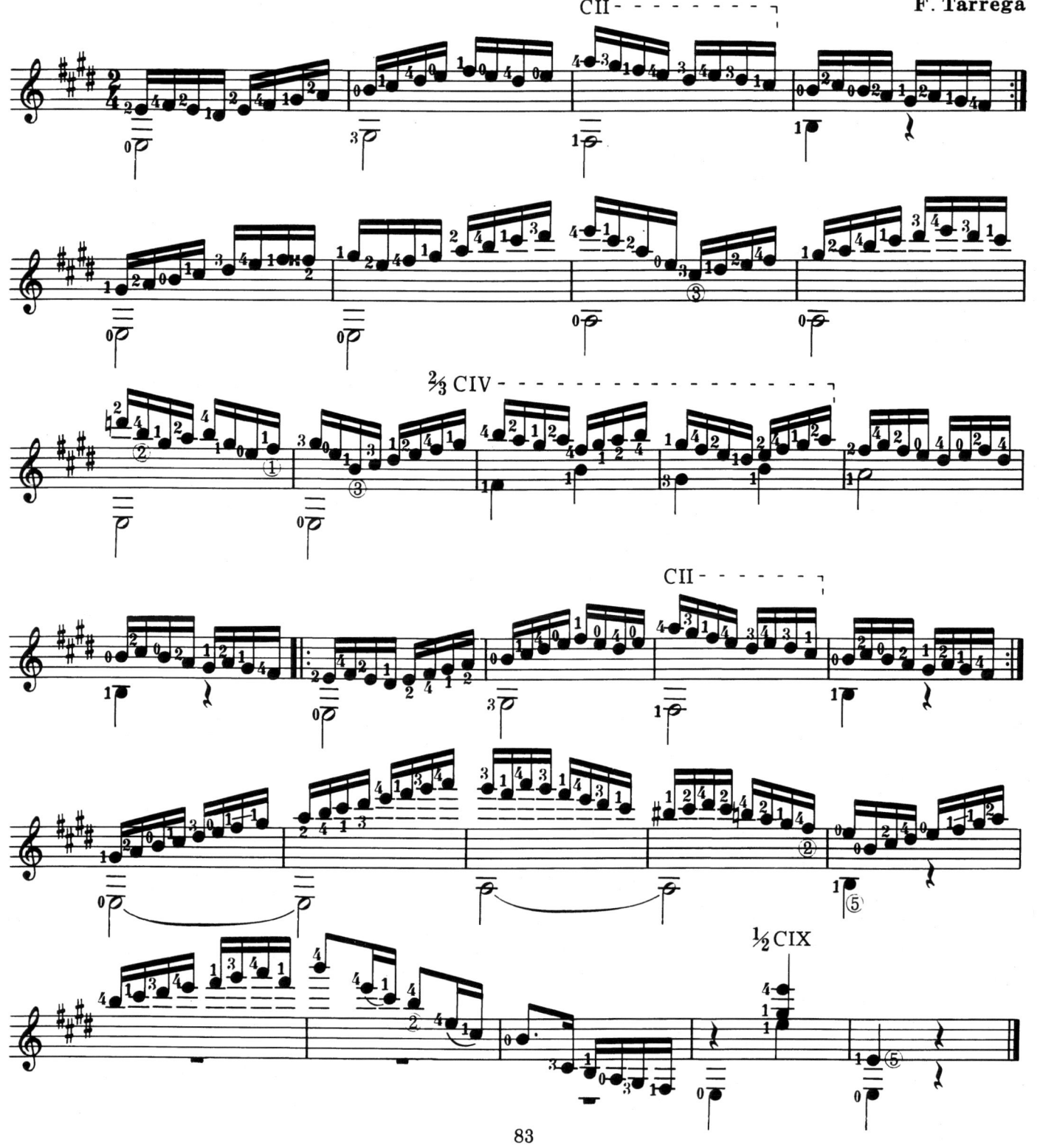

MINUET

CHORDS		SCALES	X
BARRES	⅚ full	INTERVALS	
SHIFTS		EXTENSIONS	X
SLURS		HARMONICS	

J.S. Bach

84

MINUET IN A

CHORDS		SCALES	X
BARRES	2/3 5/6 full	INTERVALS	
SHIFTS	X	EXTENSIONS	
SLURS	X	HARMONICS	

F. Tarrega

MARCH

CHORDS		SCALES	X
BARRES	½ ⅔	INTERVALS	
SHIFTS	X	EXTENSIONS	
SLURS		HARMONICS	

J.S. Bach

ALLEGRO

CHORDS		SCALES	
BARRES		INTERVALS	6th
SHIFTS		EXTENSIONS	
SLURS		HARMONICS	

F. Sor

EXERCISE

CHORDS		SCALES	
BARRES		INTERVALS	3rd
SHIFTS	X	EXTENSIONS	
SLURS		HARMONICS	

F. Carulli

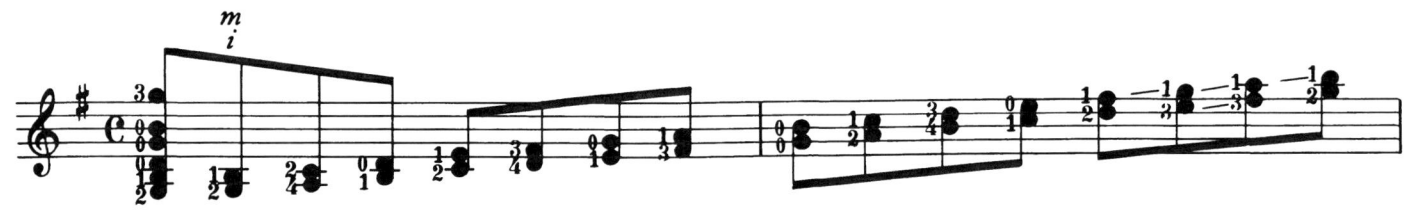

ALLEGRETTO

CHORDS		SCALES	
BARRES		INTERVALS	6th
SHIFTS	X	EXTENSIONS	
SLURS		HARMONICS	

N. Coste

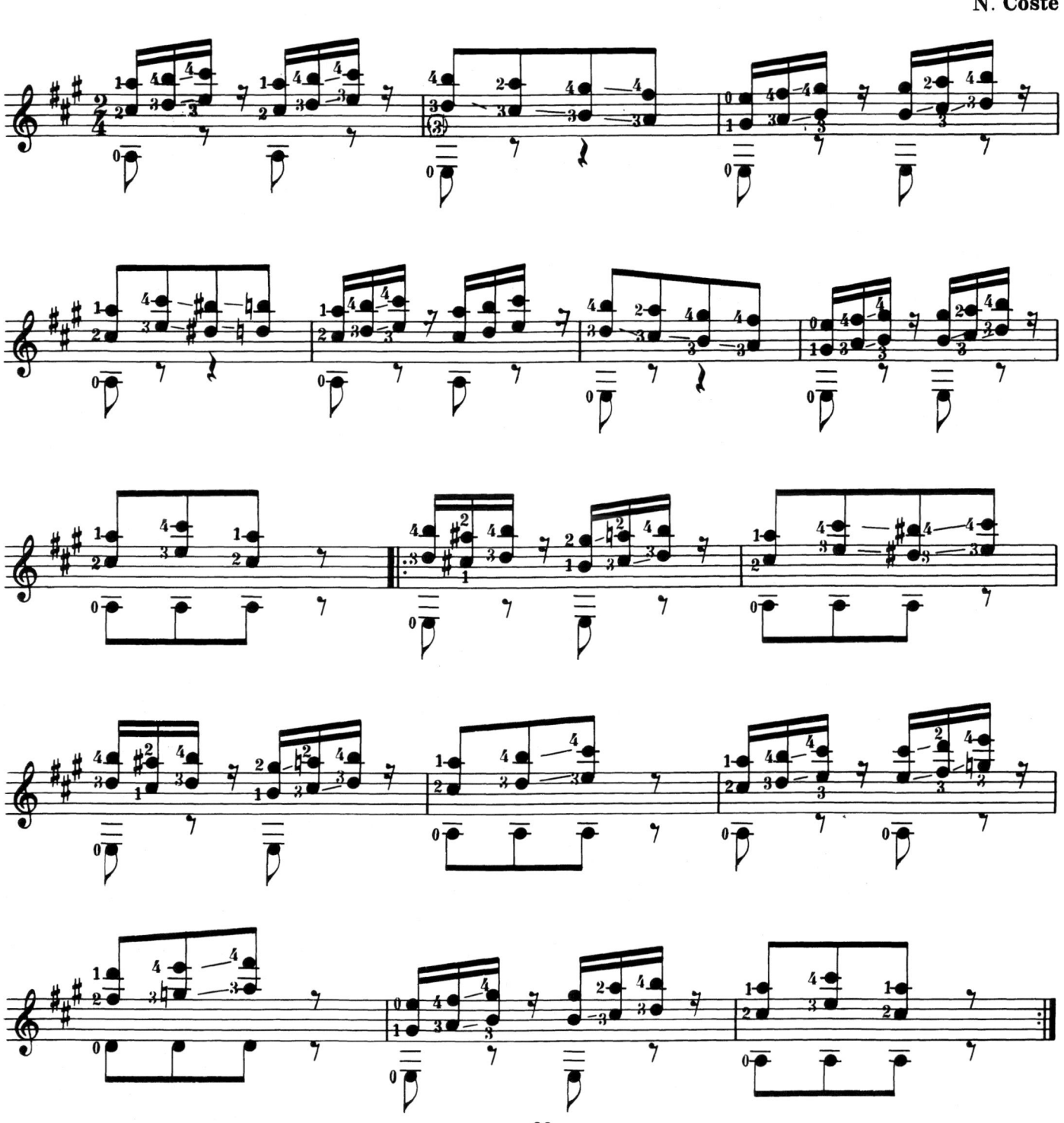

ANDANTE

CHORDS		SCALES	
BARRES		INTERVALS	3rd
SHIFTS	X	EXTENSIONS	
SLURS	X	HARMONICS	

F. Sor

MUSETTE

CHORDS			SCALES	
BARRES	2/3	full	INTERVALS	Oct.
SHIFTS			EXTENSIONS	
SLURS			HARMONICS	

J.S. Bach

PRESTISSIMO

CHORDS			SCALES	
BARRES	½	⅔	INTERVALS	3rds
SHIFTS		X	EXTENSIONS	
SLURS			HARMONICS	

M. Giuliani Op. 48 No. 3

STUDY

CHORDS		SCALES	X
BARRES	½ full	INTERVALS	
SHIFTS		EXTENSIONS	X
SLURS		HARMONICS	

D. Aguado

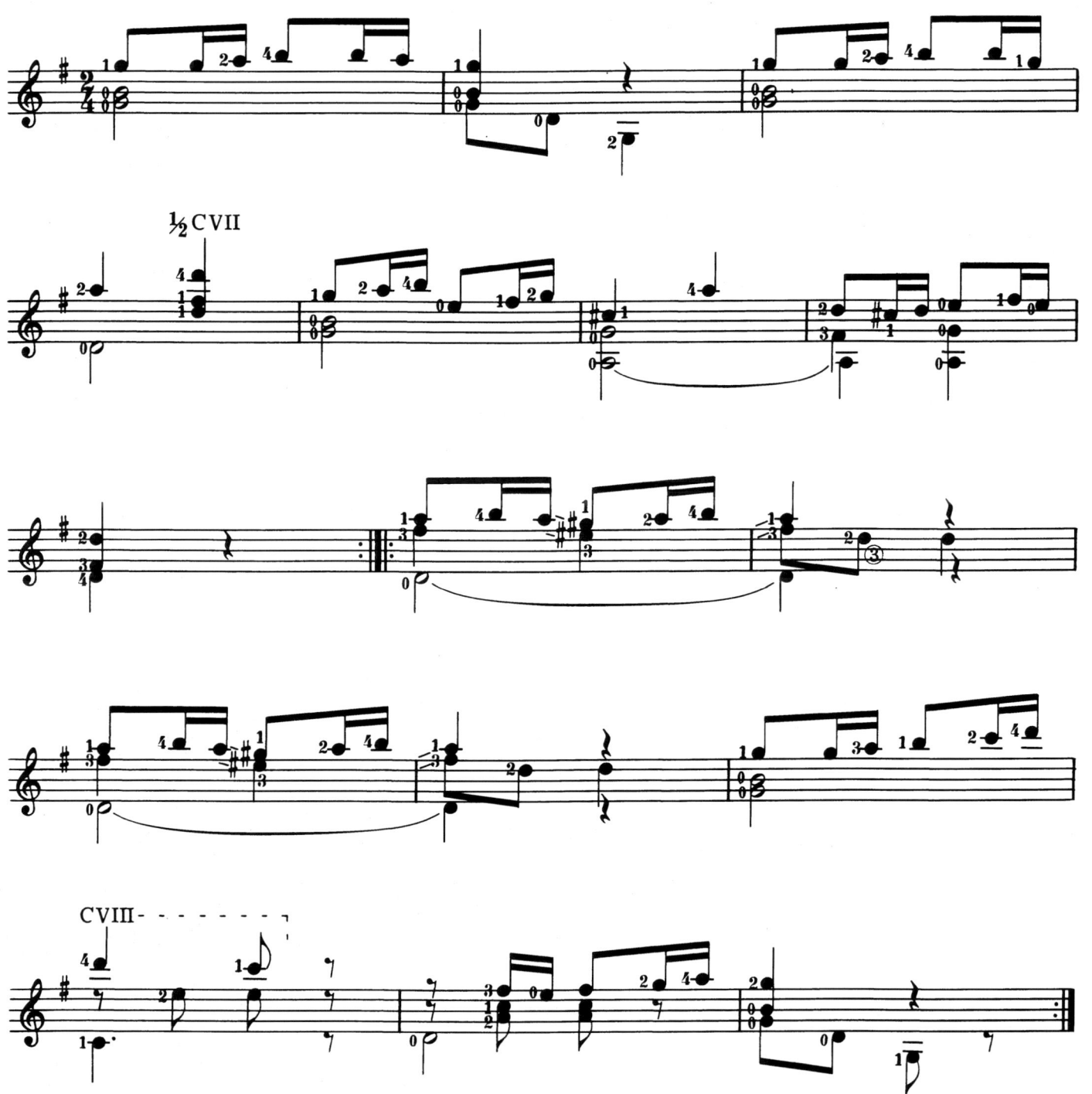

ENDECHA - OREMUS

CHORDS	X	SCALES	
BARRES	½ ⅔ ⅚	INTERVALS	
SHIFTS	X	EXTENSIONS	X
SLURS		HARMONICS	

F. Tarrega

PRELUDE

CHORDS	X	SCALES	
BARRES	⅓ ½ ⅔ ⅚	INTERVALS	
SHIFTS	X	EXTENSIONS	X
SLURS		HARMONICS	

J.S. Bach

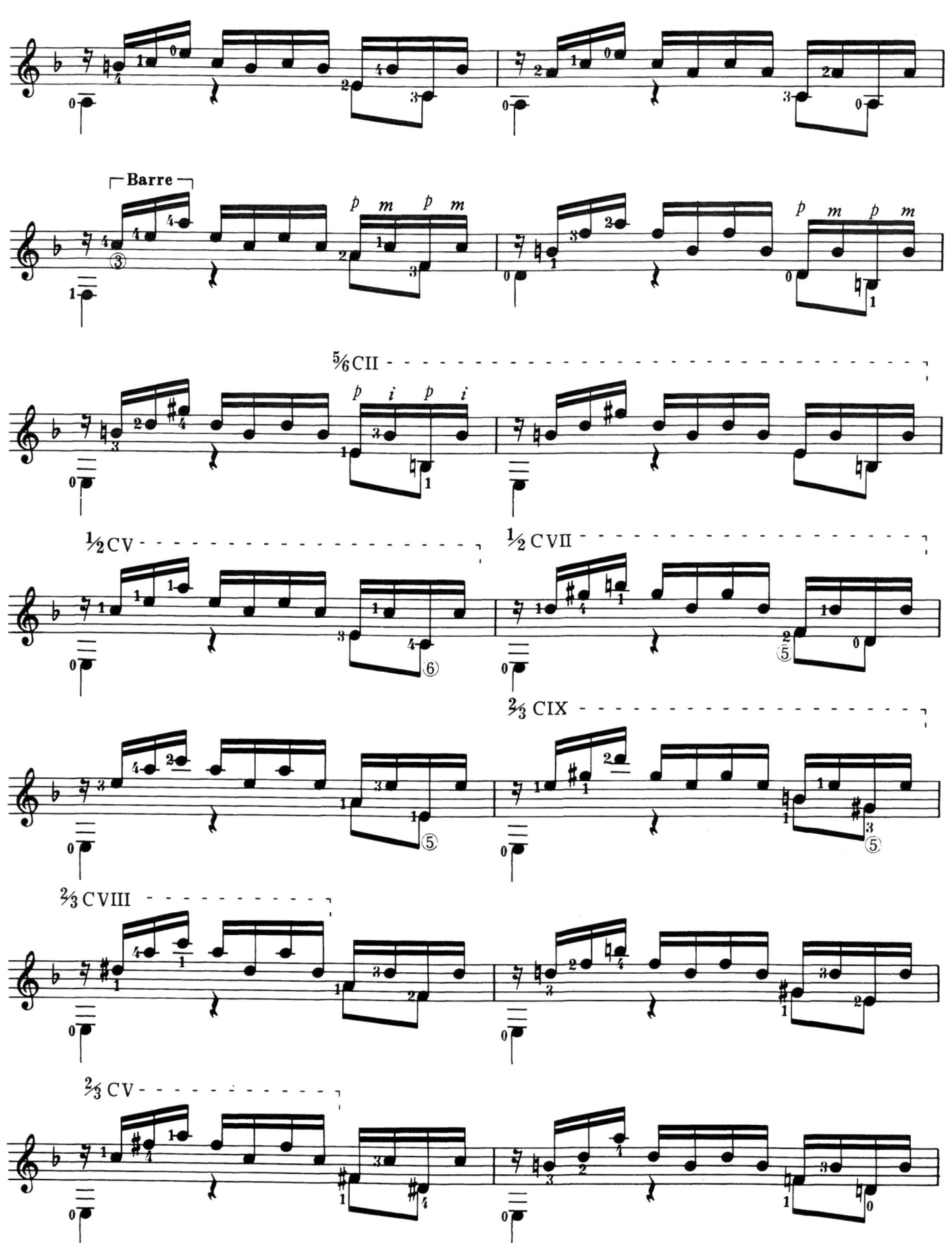

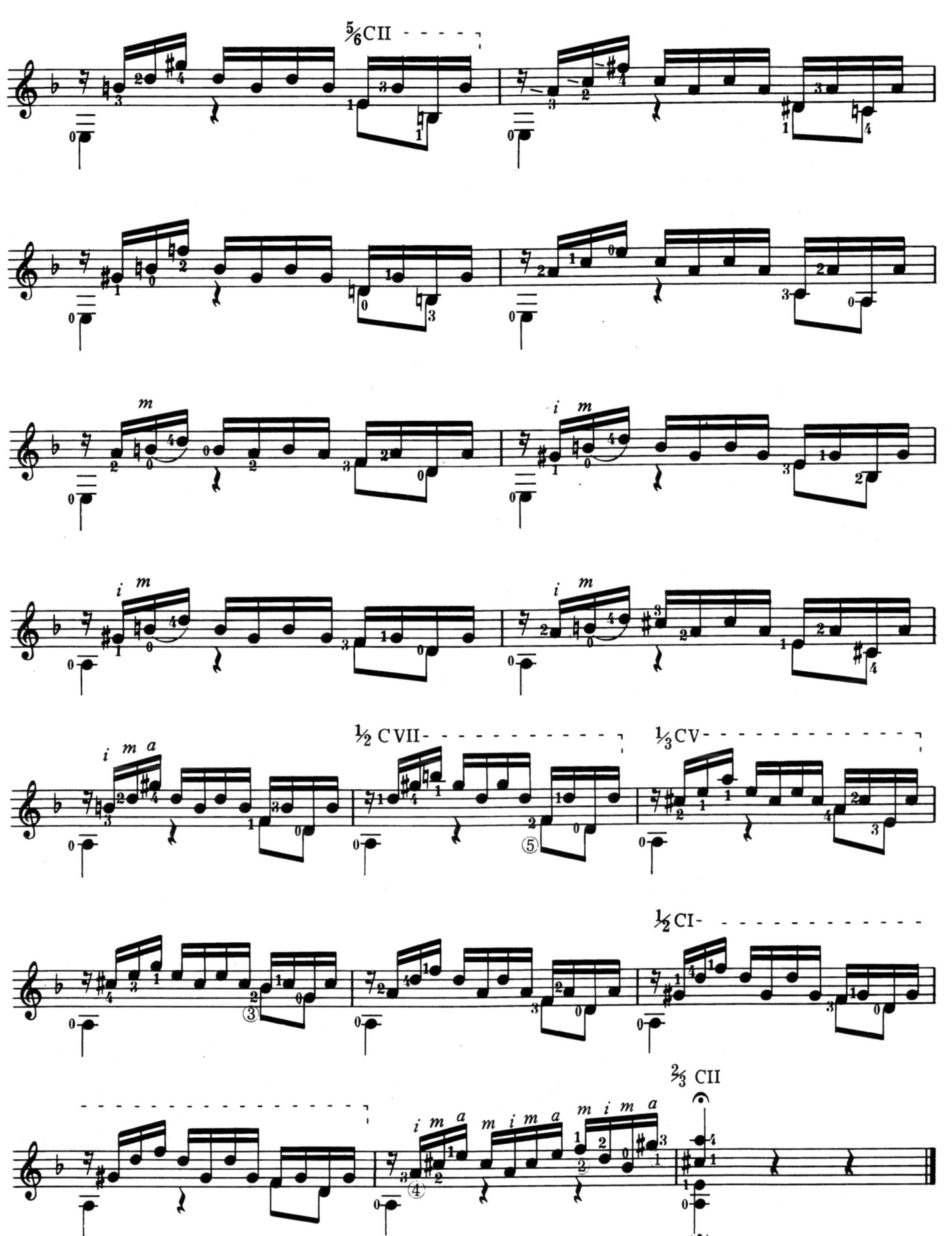

VARIATION ON AU CLAIR DE LA LUNE

CHORDS		SCALES	
BARRES		INTERVALS	
SHIFTS	X	EXTENSIONS	
SLURS		HARMONICS	X

M. Carcassi Op. 7

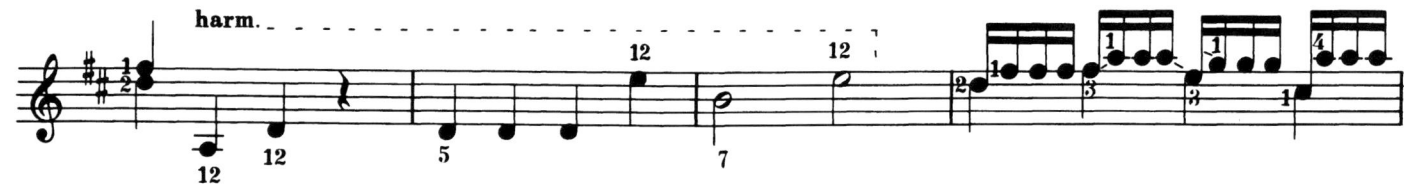

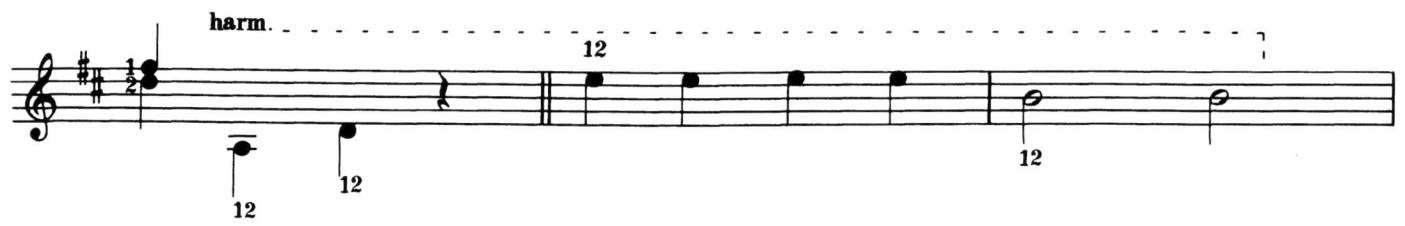

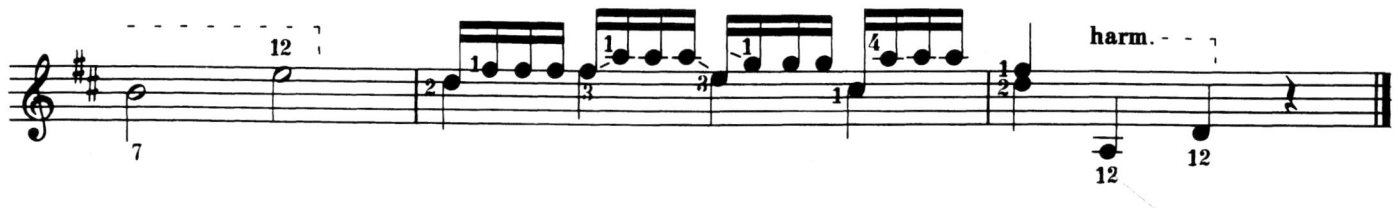

MARCHE

CHORDS		SCALES	
BARRES		INTERVALS	
SHIFTS	X	EXTENSIONS	
SLURS		HARMONICS	X

F. Sor Op. 45 No. 18

MENUET

CHORDS	X	SCALES	
BARRES	⅓ ½ ⅔ full	INTERVALS	
SHIFTS	X	EXTENSIONS	X
SLURS		HARMONICS	X

F. Sor Op. 3

MARCHE

CHORDS	X	SCALES	
BARRES	½ ⅚	INTERVALS	
SHIFTS	X	EXTENSIONS	X
SLURS		HARMONICS	X

F. Sor Op. 34

ANDANTINO GRAZIOSO

CHORDS	X	SCALES	X
BARRES	⅓ ½	INTERVALS	3rd 6th
SHIFTS	X	EXTENSIONS	X
SLURS	X	HARMONICS	

M. Carcassi Op. 5

MODERATO

CHORDS	X	SCALES	X
BARRES	½ ⅔ ⅚	INTERVALS	
SHIFTS		EXTENSIONS	X
SLURS		HARMONICS	

F. Sor Op. 31